"Some Christians have the ability to make you want to be a Christian just by be[ing...]
make the gospel alive, real, healing, and utterly attractive. I think Spencer Burke[...]
and he is sharing himself and his vision in this fine book."
—**Fr. Richard Rohr**, O.F.M., Center for Action and Contemplation, Albuque[...]

"Spencer Burke is that true friend who lovingly tells you the brutal truth about you[...]
it leads to the most important change in your life. The conversation recorded in *Making Sense of Church* is
something all Christians need to hear and church leaders dare not miss. It contains great insights for those
ready to move from chat-room rants to real-life change."
—**Chuck Smith jr.**, Senior Pastor, Capo Beach (California) Calvary, Author of *Epiphany*

"A lot of good, conceptual books and articles have been written over the last five years about the postmodern conversation among young evangelicals. But *Making Sense of Church* is the best, most revealing book
I've read on the real, ground-level dialog. For five years, theOoze.com and Spencer Burke have been at the
hub—they might even be THE cyber hub—of this communication. Listening in as Spencer interacts with this
dialog is a good read and an enjoyable journey of learning."
—**Todd Hunter**, Allelon Community of Churches, Former National Director, Vineyard-USA

"In the face of a growing sense that the standard evangelical approach is not working, heated conversations
are springing up—it's a time of fertile ferment. TheOoze.com—and this book's distillation of its conversations—
focuses on some of those conversations and points to solutions. *Making Sense of Church* is an engaging, stimulating presentation of bubbling new ideas at the very moment of their birth."
—**Frederica Mathewes-Green**, Author of *Facing East*, www.frederica.com

"It's rare that a person writes a book to explain his obsession. It's rare that a person's obsession is to explore
the complexity of how a 2,000-plus-year old body called the church is navigating a series of tectonic
changes in the global culture. Some obsessions are more interesting, more complex, and more urgent than
others. This book ranks high on all counts. *Making Sense of Church* is neither a prophetic diatribe nor a
happy-faced cheer book about the church and its culture. It's a serious reflection from a man who sits in the
center of many conversations about the topic and knows better than to attempt a neatly tied solution. It
allows the reader to enter into the confusion and emerge unscathed in the body—but changed in the heart.
It will result in a greater depth of understanding of a very complex issue and a greater hope in God's character as the One who is controlling the affairs of both the church and the culture."
—**Brad Smith**, Executive Director, International Urban Associates

"Nine times the gospels record Jesus as saying, "He who has ears to hear, hear." This book is the best listening post out there to hear the authentic voice of the future in its cries for God."
—**Leonard Sweet**, Drew University, George Fox University, preachingplus.com

"Spencer, if the only reason you've devoted so much of your money, time, and energy to TheOoze.com was
to write *Making Sense of Church*, then it was worth it. Truly, this book has helped me understand part of the
journey I've traveled in the last 10 years. TheOoze.com message board contributions and your authentic
and vulnerable narrative illustrate the current transition that the North American church faces. Thanks for your
attempt at making sense of church in the postmodern era."
—**Charlie Wear**, Publisher, *Next-Wave* Web magazine and fellow traveler on the journey with Jesus

"Bulletin boards like TheOoze.com are where the emerging church was birthed, and *Making Sense of
Church* is like sneaking into the maternity ward."
—**Tony Jones**, Author of *Soul Shaper: Exploring Spirituality and Contemplative Practices in Youth
Ministry* (Youth Specialties)

"Spencer Burke is a hospitable guy, and when you experience his hospitality, you're guaranteed to learn a
lot. He's been throwing 'learning parties' around the country and online for the last several years, and now,
through *Making Sense of Church*, you can experience the next best thing to being there. This is an under-
standable and enjoyable onramp to the emerging church conversation."
—**Brian D. McLaren**, Pastor (crcc.org), Author of *A New Kind of Christian*, senior fellow in emergent
(emergentvillage.com)

"*Making Sense of Church* is a unique contribution to the study of the emerging church in a postmodern cultural context. Spencer Burke is in direct contact on a daily basis with the people we need to hear from
through his highly acclaimed Web site. The posts are riveting, and Spencer's commentary provides penetrat-
ing analysis."
—**Eddie Gibbs**, The Donald A. McGavran Professor of Church Growth, School of World Mission,
Fuller Theological Seminary, Author of *ChurchNext: Quantum Changes in How We Do Ministry*

"If anyone has not only an ear, but an eye, mind, and heart tuned into the conversations of the emerging church, it's Spencer Burke. *Making Sense of Church* will bring you into the very questions, ponderings, frustrations, and joys of those rethinking and reimagining the church."
—**Dan Kimball**, Author of *The Emerging Church: Vintage Christianity for New Generations*
  (emergentYS), Pastor, Vintage Faith Church, Santa Cruz, California

"Spencer is one of the youngest, freshest minds I know. I love his ideas—they challenge me to think."
—**Kenton Beshore**, Senior Pastor, Mariners Church, Irvine, California

"Congrats, Spencer. You've just opened up a brand-new window on ministry in the postmodern transition: from information, positioning, and image to essence, presence, and transparence. Your combination of humility and winsome truth-telling gives the most skeptical leaders permission to find themselves in your journey."
—**Sally Morgenthaler**, Sacramentis.com, author of *Worship Evangelism*

"Love the book. The warrior-to-gardener metaphor is a needed transition for church in a security age. The thing I like most about *Making Sense of Church* is that it gives voice to those not usually heard. It lets the young people themselves speak out rather than attempting to speak for them."
—**Andrew Jones**, The Boaz Project, Prague, Czech Republic

"What a great read. Not only the thoughts of one man but also the contributions of many make it impossible to ignore the aspirations of those who love God with all their hearts but have found the church of Jesus a hard place to grow up. The key at this time is that we start to think differently. Spencer Burke's use of changing metaphors gives us new pictures to look at and new thoughts to think. Those who have ears or eyes— look and listen!"
—**Billy Kennedy**, Team Leader, Community Church, Southampton, U.K.

"Finding new metaphors has become an urgent task of the young leaders concerned about ministry in a postmodern world. Spencer Burke and Colleen Pepper are masters at capturing the new images, symbols, and words that express the journey into the future. They provide us with handles to walk the journey, and they do so with unforgettable color and challenging imagery."
—**Robert Webber**, Myers Professor of Ministry, Northern Seminary, Author of *The Younger Evangelicals*

"Spencer Burke is the right man at the right place at the right time. He enjoys a ringside seat in the dramatic dialog between the church of history and the church of post-history. He stands in the middle— between where God has been and where God is going. No iconoclast, Burke embraces both past and future while challenging the dead metaphors of a passing culture and the overnight clichés of the new 'cool' culture. Throughout *Making Sense of Church*, he blows away church leaders at both ends of the spectrum with the 'extreme reality' of a loving Christ."
—**Thomas Hohstadt**, Author of *Dying to Live*, FutureChurch.net

"For all those confused about where the church is going and what we should be doing about it, *Making Sense of Church* is a big help. It's a sensible rapprochement between established churches and the emerging churches of the 21st century."
—**Tony Campolo**, Professor of Sociology, Eastern University

"Spencer Burke invites us to invest ourselves in the challenging work of reexamining what it means to be a Christ-follower in a new postmodern culture. This book is must-reading for all those in both the emerging and the established church who want to create authentic new expressions of life, church, and mission."
—**Tom Sine**, Author of *Living on Purpose* and *Mustard Seed Vs McWorld*

Making Sense of Church

Making Sense of Church

Eavesdropping on Emerging Conversations about God, Community, and Culture

by **Spencer Burke**
with **Colleen Pepper**

emergent
ys

www.emergentys.com

ZONDERVAN™

WWW.ZONDERVAN.COM

Edited by David Sanford

To my father, Bob Burke, who taught me to risk believing that anything is possible—including a midlife career change! And to my mother, Claire Burke, who showed me what it means to be compassionate and gracious at all times.

Contents

Acknowledgments

Spencer Burke

Remember Joshua 4:6? It's where God tells the Israelites to pick up 12 stones and build a monument. Why? So that they'll always remember their crossing of the Jordan River into the Promised Land. The monument not only honors God's faithfulness in their lives, but also helps them to share their story with their children and grandchildren.

In many ways, that's what this book is for me—it's a marker on my own personal journey with God. These last five years have been quite an adventure. Crazy, chaotic, and confusing—yet wonderfully rewarding as well.

To my wife, Lisa, your love and encouragement have kept me going when nothing else could. You are my harmony. For your patience and understanding, your wisdom and strength, thank you.

To my son, Alden, thank you for sharing your Dad with the world and showing me what it means to live life to the fullest. Your adventuresome spirit and genuine love for people never cease to amaze me.

To my daughter, Grace, your courage and "fight" have taught me to live in the moment. Your smile and giggle is a constant reminder of God's hand.

To my extended family, thanks for walking with Lisa and I through all the crazymaking of our life together. Your support means the world to us. Dave, for your thoughtful review of the manuscript, and Jan, for your generous support—for all the time you've both given to our family—I'm truly grateful.

I want to also thank those people who've journeyed alongside me over the years and whose personalities and stories have, in some way, added to the flavor of this book: Jack Hafer, Ray Botello, Leila Birch, Grace Spencer, Ralph Didier, Jim Burns, Kenton Beshore, Don Hendricks, and Ron Jensen.

Then there are newer friends—individuals who have crossed my path more recently and have faithfully encouraged me to keep on keeping on: Todd Hunter, Brian McLaren, Jason Evans, Joe Myers, Malcolm Hawker, Dave Trotter, Matt and Krista Palmer, Alan Hartung, Ray Levesque, Charlie Ware, Jordan Cooper, Joshua Dunford and Team Burnkit, and Ray Majoran.

To Mark Oestreicher, thank you for believing in me and giving me an opportunity to find my voice. While I was thinking many writers, you were thinking one: me.

To Dave Urbanski at YS, and David Sanford, our editor, your wisdom and expertise have made this a stronger book in every respect.

To Phyllis Jelinek and Kim Storm, you were there when the going got tough. You helped me to get many of my stories down on paper so I could take the next steps. My sincere thanks.

To Colleen Pepper, your keen ability to take my thousands of ideas and shape them into a coherent whole is incredible. I love what we're able to do together and trust this will be the first of many projects for us.

To the new explorers I've met through ETREK—Todd, David, Rod, Tony, Rodney, Stew, Randy, and Bill—it's been an honor and privilege to journey with you.

And most of all, to TheOoze.com community—both those who came alongside me in the early days and those who are actively sharing in the conversation today—my sincere thanks. It's comforting to know that I'm not the only crazy one out there. This book is a tribute to you all.

Colleen Pepper

Joshua honored the Israelites' journey by piling up stones from the Jordan. As for me, I think I'll use manuscript pages.

It's pretty crazy to think how this all came about. Kara, if not for you, my friendship with Spencer might never have happened. Your invitation to lunch gave me the opportunity to shake the man's hand and shamelessly plug my services. Wow. That's all I can say.

To Terry Mattingly, thanks for believing in me and encouraging me to make writing a career. That summer in Washington, D.C., changed my life.

To my fellow freelancers, Fred, Louise, and Susanna, we've survived the "wilderness"—the Promised Land awaits.

To Pastor Bill and Christ the King Presbyterian Church, you've blessed me more than you'll ever know. The gospel has never been more real to me.

To Lorna, God is good. Very good. Thank you for everything.

To my husband, Jeremy, you're amazing. I couldn't ask for a better cheerleader. You not only remind me of God's incredible love and grace, you lavish it upon me—day after day after day.

And finally, to Spencer, it's been a wild and wonderful ride. Thank you so much for the opportunity.

Foreword

"I wish I had never seen the Ring! Why did it come to me? Why was I chosen?" laments Frodo, upon learning the true identity of the mysterious inheritance that has come his way. In response, the old wizard, Gandalf, offers a wise appraisal: "Such questions cannot be answered...You may be sure that it was not for any merit that others do not possess: not for power or wisdom, at any rate. But you have been chosen, and you must therefore use such strength and heart and wits as you have."

In encouraging Queen Esther to act on behalf of the Jews—whose lives were being threatened by Xerxes' decree— Mordecai offers similar counsel. He asks rhetorically, "Who knows but that you have come to royal position for such a time as this?" (Esther 4:14).

We are living in confusing times. Many culture-watchers are convinced that our society is undergoing a transformation of broad proportions. This cultural shift goes by various designations. Some observers tell us we are in the throes of a transition from a Christian to a post-Christian era. Others declare we are moving from a Constantinian to a post-Constantinian situation. But the most widely used description suggests we are witnessing the emergence of a "postmodern" society. Whatever may be the preferred nomenclature, the various voices are in agreement that the cultural shift now transpiring carries grave implications for the church.

Confusing times...transitional times. Both call for a wise response. To date, however, wisdom has not always prevailed. In their enthusiasm for all things postmodern, some Christians throw caution to the wind and uncritically hail the postmodern turn as the panacea for everything that ails the church. More widespread, however, is a quite different response. For other Christians pronounce an undiscerning anathema on anything postmodern, even railing against the postmodern condition as the chief enemy of the faith today. Some go so far as to advocate a holy war against whatever they deem to be even remotely "postmodern," often doing so in the name of preserving the values of modernity or with the hope of returning to a long-lost, idyllic premodern situation.

Like every social ethos, the postmodern condition is a mixed bag. Although it does harbor problematic dimensions that pose potential hazards, the postmodern turn is no more of a problem to the church than the modern condition was—or the premodern, for that matter. For this reason, admitting that the postmodern turn is not a cure-all does not give us license to treat it as a problem needing to be solved. Instead Christians would do well to view the emerging context simply as an opportunity to be carefully and judiciously appropriated.

Appropriating the postmodern condition in a manner that can advance the gospel within the contemporary context is demanding work. It can only be accomplished as we engage in extended conversations with one another about matters crucial to the faith—conversations such as the ones occurring on Web sites such as TheOoze.com and found within the pages of *Making Sense of Church*. Moreover, truly beneficial conversations should invite us to explore new metaphors that can assist us in revisioning who we are as the fellowship of Christ's disciples called to be a witnessing community within the emerging postmodern context—metaphors such as the ones developed in the pages of this book.

But launching into such engagement requires, above all, that we gain a profound sense that we have been chosen, that we have been given a royal position as those called to be Christ's people—for a time such as this. And seeking to be the church in a seemingly post-Christian, post-Constantinian, postmodern society requires that we use such strength and heart and wits as we have. In this crucial task of seeking to think wisely about our calling in the emerging context, Spencer Burke and Colleen Pepper stand not only as examples but also as mentors.

—*Stanley J. Grenz, Pioneer McDonald Professor, Carey Theological College, Vancouver, B.C.*

Introduction

Whenever I'm asked to describe this book, I'm never quite sure what to say. Is it about postmodernism and the church? My own personal journey in ministry? Conversations from TheOoze message boards?

The fact is, it's all these things and more.

Five years ago, I left the established church. I gave up my job as a pastor at one of the largest churches in America to go...well, nowhere (except my garage-turned-office). Naturally, the people around me were confused. "Spencer, what are you doing? Why are you doing this? What about your family? What about ministry?"

When I started focusing my energies on TheOoze.com, there were many audible sighs of relief. Phew! At least I was doing something constructive with my time. And yet, still, people around me were puzzled. What was the big deal about postmodernism anyway? What was it that I had become so passionate about? And why was I suddenly spending so much time online?

In many ways, this book is the answer to those questions. It's a letter, of sorts, back to my friends in the established church. Five years into the journey, this is where I'm at.

It's also my attempt to help bring much-needed understanding between those who would call themselves "emerging" and the rest of the church. I don't know about you, but my heart sinks every time I hear "us vs. them" rhetoric. This book is not a commercial for a postmodern church. It's not a slam against the established church. It's simply about the questions, hopes, and fears of real people.

Scan through a chapter and you'll notice that much of the content comes from visitors to TheOoze.com message boards—men and women who, like all of us, are struggling to understand what the gospel means in today's postmodern culture. In the age of "reality television," this is a "reality book." The messages are raw and to the point. While they've been edited for length, as well as for spelling and punctuation (for clarity), in most cases they appear largely as they do online. No doubt you'll cheer for some and boo others.

To those of you who are looking for answers—programs to copy and steps to complete—this book will likely leave you disappointed. I'm afraid we offer you explorations more than destinations. In my experience, there are no shortcuts, no quick fixes. Journeying with God is exactly that: a journey. Frustratingly long at times, and yet joyously rewarding as well.

At this point in my life, I continue to find myself pulled in two different directions. My "established church" friends question why I spend so much time with people who, they believe, have given up on truth—people who, they say, have sold out the gospel for the sake of culture. "And besides," they ask, "isn't postmodernism just a passing phase?" I can't help but wonder if I hear fear in their voices. Try as they might, one question continues to haunt this group: "What if we're wrong?"

My "emerging church" friends, meanwhile, sometimes seem more angry than fearful. "Why don't you cut your old church friends loose?" they ask, their frustration evident. "You're not a part of that world any longer. Don't even waste your breath. Why bother trying to argue with them or convince them? The gospel is moving ahead and we need to move with it." They feel as though they haven't been heard or supported in their journey.

The need for a bridge between these camps seems obvious. My hope is that this book might in some way usher in a new era of dialogue. An era where we can have meaningful, compassionate conversations with each other, no matter where our allegiances lie—modern or postmodern, Eastern Orthodox or Catholic, megachurch or house church.

If not a bridge, then I pray this book will at least be a catalyst for change in your own life. I trust it will give you an opportunity to think though your own personal spirituality and wrestle with what it means to follow Jesus Christ in the twenty-first century. Who knows? At the end of it, you may find your life takes a turn in a dramatic new direction. Or, then again, perhaps not.

Perhaps you'll simply find that you have more in common with other people than you ever thought possible—and that, in itself, will be revolutionary. In any case, I invite you to dive in and risk seeing the world in a new way.

Reality Check

Metaphors for Transition

chapter 1

The word "postmodern" first appeared in the Oxford English Dictionary in 1949. Postmodern is what's come about after—and often in reaction to—modernism, which dominated Western thought for a majority of the twentieth century. In recent decades, every major sphere of life has evolved to become postmodern—movies, literature, art, architecture, business, politics. Everything, that is, except "The Church."

In many ways, the church is the last bastion of modernism in our culture. It's not that the church hasn't changed over the years, but the changes have been cosmetic. We've unplugged organs, padded pews, removed shag carpet, and added video projectors. Meanwhile, everything else in our culture has undergone a complete metamorphosis. The changes are so radical that some parts of our culture are barely recognizable to modern eyes.

The world has changed

Been to a movie lately? Forget linear, moralistic plots. Instead, films like *Memento* and *Being John Malkovich* and newer releases continue to push the limits of visual storytelling. Bizarre, brain-twisting movies, these films demand their viewers to create meaning for themselves. Locations and time frames are deliberately ambiguous. Characters are complex contradictions—a fascinating mix of good, evil, and things in between.

The same can be said of postmodern literature. In the past fifty years, a new character has emerged: the antihero. No longer can we assume that the good guy will win in the end. Such expectations seem nostalgic, if not painfully naïve. In our experience, the world just doesn't work like that.

What about business? We've come to accept that profits, not people, are the ultimate priority. Corporate downsizing has become an everyday occurrence.

Chances of working for the same company for forty years and someday picking up a gold watch for your trouble are slim. Can you imagine 1950s TV dad Ward Cleaver ever losing his job? I didn't think so. In today's world, though, nothing is certain. Dot coms are here today and gone tomorrow. Hostile takeovers are a way of life, and strategic mergers an apparent necessity. The landscape continuously shifts, and only those who adapt quickly seem to survive.

Our politics have shifted, too. Criticize big government in the 1950s and a sweaty senator from Wisconsin might interrogate you on national television and brand you a traitor. In the 1960s, however, the rules began to change. Sit-ins and protests paved the way for a greater degree of free speech. Today, we're able to protest to our hearts' content. Why? Because we've come to see just how fallible our leaders are. History has shown us that U.S. presidents, in spite of their power and prestige, still manage to lie and lust like everyone else. We no longer have illusions about these things. As a country, we've come to distrust authority, recognizing instead that our nation is indeed capable of getting involved in unjust wars, and that we, too, have the potential to oppress people in other countries for our own economic gain. The divine right of kings—or authority figures, in general—is dead. We've seen too much.

The reality is, postmodernism is not a fad. It's not a hot new trend we can ride out and ignore. Whether or not you realize it, you live in a postmodern world—and you have been living in it for quite some time! It's like Madge, the Palmolive lady, used to say: "You're soaking in it." There's no point in pretending that you're not— or wishing that things would go back to the way they were thirty years ago. They can't; you can't. No fountain of youth exists.

The challenge, of course, is determining what all of this means for the church and knowing how to move forward. What does it mean to be postmodern and Christian? If such a combination is possible, then what does a "postmodern church" look like? And just how far are we willing to go in unwrapping the evangelical package?

Rising to the challenge

Oddly enough, Jesus found himself at the center of a similar cultural debate. Remember the discussion about whether God's people should pay taxes to Caesar? Forever trying to trip up Jesus, the religious leaders of the day sent out men to challenge him on his obedience to the law.

"Teacher," they said, "we know that you speak and teach what is right and are not influenced by what others think. You sincerely teach the ways of God. Now tell us—is it right to pay taxes to the Roman government or not?" (Luke 20:21–22 NLT). What does Jesus do? He asks them to show him a coin. "Whose picture and title are stamped on it?" Upon hearing their answer, "Caesar's," he simply replies, "Well then, give to Caesar what belongs to him. But everything that belongs to God must be given to God."

It's crazy, really. Considering that Jesus could make coins appear anywhere he wanted, including inside a fish's mouth (Matthew 17:24–27), did he really need to give an answer to this question? Since it's all God's, why not tell these people off, or just ignore them and move on?

Perhaps Jesus was making a point about respecting the culture in which we live. In a wonderful, sarcastic and playful way, Jesus affirmed his deity while acknowledging the reality of life on planet Earth. True, this world is not our home, so we don't necessarily have to play by its rules, but we may choose to do so for the cause of Jesus Christ. Yet in doing so, we may sometimes find ourselves at odds with other Christians.

I find it interesting that Jesus instructed the people to figure out what was Caesar's. In most of life, that's not as easy as it sounds. The more I think about Jesus' statement, the more convinced I become that taking a hard look at our lives is actually biblical. As I see it, postmodernism provides an unprecedented opportunity for self-examination. By its very nature, postmodernism offers us a chance to think long and hard about why we do the things we do. It forces us to wrestle with our beliefs and our traditions, our programs and our theology, all in an effort to uncover those aspects of our faith that are really and truly God's—and, by extension, those that are not.

Still, the concept of deconstruction is a scary one. We get nervous at the thought of deconstructing anything—primarily because we're afraid if we pull our religion apart, we may end up with nothing in the end. We picture home repair projects gone wrong—with heaven or hell hanging in the balance. Never mind an angry spouse. What if we aren't able to fit the pieces back together in any kind of coherent whole? What then?

I guess that's why I prefer to use the words "unwrap" or "unpackage." As Christians responding to the challenge of postmodernism, we're not attacking our faith, we're simply unpackaging it. We're daring to pull off the shells of sentiment and tradition in confidence of finding a pearl of great price inside. We've lived long enough to suspect that maybe, just maybe, some of what appears to have Jesus' face on it actually may be Caesar's. Whereas postmodern secularists may deconstruct everything down to its essence, postmodern Christians ultimately will retain at least one absolute, Jesus Christ.

Playing by new rules

I think it's important to understand, too, that postmodernism isn't just about critiquing modernism. Whether or not we realize it, some of what we've called "doctrines" or "truths" over the years are, in fact, cultural interpretations. In many ways, many of the church's messages today are similar but far from identical to those preached by Martin Luther. By the same token, the messages preached by Luther were similar but certainly not identical to those upheld by Constantine.

Our understanding of Christianity has morphed and changed down through the centuries, in large part dependent on the church's cultural contexts. Political and economic factors always have shaped our understanding. As a result, I believe we need to risk exposing some of our most cherished beliefs to the light, trusting that no matter whose face is revealed on the coin, we'll be able to continue the journey.

While examining our beliefs and practices is a good start, any serious evaluation of our faith also must challenge our subconscious beliefs. Business author Peter Senge writes of mental models—the "deeply ingrained assumptions, generalizations or even pictures or images that influence how we understand the world and how we take action." In his book *The Fifth Discipline*, Senge points out how powerful these images can be. "The problem with mental models arises," he says, "when the models are tacit—when they exist below the level of awareness."

Many new insights fail to get put into practice in business—or in the church—because they conflict with these deeply held internal images of how the world works, images that limit us to familiar ways of thinking and acting.

While looking at our theology and systems is good, our churches won't ultimately change if we don't also examine our mental models—the metaphors that guide us in our everyday life. Our mental models often prove more powerful than anything else floating around in our heads. Think about it. How many churches have warm, fuzzy mission statements full of words like compassionate, caring, and committed—yet call their people to take up arms against a godless, secular culture?

Because of this fact, Leonard Sweet actually advocates adopting "image statements"—pictures that stimulate us to action and capture the essence of who we are and who we want to become. Rather than writing convoluted mission and vision statements, which often contradict our tacit "mental models," he suggests that churches begin to rally around a single image.

Sweet's own personal image statement, for instance, is a child on a swing. "As a historian of Christianity, I want the church to lean back—not just back to the '50s, but all the way back through 2000 years of history," Sweet writes. "All the way back until we're, in the words of that Sunday school song, 'Leaning, Leaning, Leaning on the Everlasting Arms.' But at the same time, and I do mean simultaneously, we must use that energy and power that comes from 'learning to lean' to kick forward into the future and Carpe Manana."

Exploring new ideas

Sweet's swing is a powerful image for what's beginning to happen in churches all over North America, and certainly what's happening every day on TheOoze.com. Each week, thousands of people visit the Website hoping to come to a deeper understanding of what postmodernism means for them and their particular spiritual communities. Many log onto TheOoze's message boards—a virtual water cooler—to share thoughts, observations, and questions with one another.

This book captures some of that discussion. It gives you a chance to listen in on the dialogue as it happens—to eavesdrop, in a sense, as people wrestle and unpack everything from styles of worship to the finer points of evangelical theology. Of course, we can't include every message or every thread. So at times you may hear only bits and pieces of a conversation. Nevertheless, I believe these snippets can help prompt your thinking and broaden your perspective. They're critical pieces in a terribly complex puzzle.

I also have incorporated many of my own thoughts throughout the text. In fact, each chapter begins with a narrative from my own life, as well as a discussion about mental models—the images that have guided the church to this point, and the images that I believe may guide us in the future. Although each chapter builds on previous chapters, they also stand alone, so don't feel like you have to read this book in any particular order. Scan the table of contents again and then jump in at the point that most interests you.

Having said that, I do hope you'll take the time to read the entire book and consider each of the chapters with an open mind. Be forewarned. This book is not an easy read. You may not agree with everything that is said. Some posts may offend you slightly; others may strike you as downright heretical. But persevere!

One of my goals in writing this book is to create opportunities for people in the established church to connect with those who are "emerging"—to create a common vocabulary between us so that we can move forward together as one body, the body of Jesus Christ.

I can't stress that last point enough. As I travel around from conference to conference, and from church to church, I'm discouraged by the amount of "us and them" rhetoric that I hear. I don't know that we do ourselves any favors by getting into one more fight over biblical inerrancy or over five-point Calvinism. Yet, for years, that's exactly what our conversations have continued to revolve around. We've doggedly kept trying to define and redefine ourselves by what we do and do not believe.

The language of metaphor offers us a much-needed alternative.

Let me say it again: This book is not an argument about theology. It's not even a philosophical discussion. It's simply a conversation. It's a conversation about church—The Church.

Listen in—and then let me know what you think. You can post your opinions, rants, or raves, and experience the expanding converstion by logging on to www.MakingSenseofChurch.com.

Chapter 2

Tour Guide to Traveler
A Conversation about "Leadership"

In the summer of 1980, I needed a job. Home from college and desperate to make some money, I soon found myself wearing a white button-down shirt, swinging a microphone, and driving trams of tourists around old Sacramento: "On your left, the famous riverfront. On your right, the historic train museum."

Interestingly enough, ten years later I was still running tours for a living— not of Sacramento, but of Christian Spirituality. As a teaching pastor at a megachurch, I was responsible to help people move along in their spiritual journey—to help them get from Point A to Point B and eventually to heaven.

Every now and then, I also had the privilege of showing them out-of-the-way places. Sites like Forest Home, the very camp where Sunday school teacher Henrietta Mears challenged Billy Graham and Bill Bright to go change the world. Talk about an evangelical Kodak moment.

In 1993, we held our annual men's retreat at Forest Home and I not only sat where Billy Graham sat, but I also had the opportunity to speak into the lives of 500 men. Guided meditations, small group discussions—we did it all. At the end of the weekend, we gathered the group for a big, "bang-the-drum" wrap-up session. As part of this time, we opened the mic and invited participants to share and encourage one another.

I can't remember everyone who spoke during that open mic session. I can't remember who went first or second or third. I actually remember what only one man said. Why? Because something he said touched me at a level so deep I thought it might destroy me.

He talked about his relationship with his father and about all the time he had spent that year processing his childhood to make peace with his past. He told of missed baseball games and forgotten birthdays, longed-for hugs and overlooked trophies. It was like listening to Harry Chapin's "Cat's in the Cradle"—the story of a father who didn't have time for his son and the son who grew up to return the favor.

The more he talked, the more I identified with his story. Then he threw a sharp-breaking curve ball: "I've come to see that actually I've been the guilty one," he said. "All those things I thought were issues with my father were really about me."

What?

My heart pounded. My chin began to quiver. My breathing became labored. He was telling my story—except the last part. This man had found freedom from his past, healing from the wounds of childhood, and a peace that I knew nothing about. Simply put, he'd been able to forgive.

All the pain I had so carefully stuffed in the depths of my heart began rushing to the surface. My face was hot; my palms were sweaty. At that moment, I had two options. Would I continue to be a tour guide, somehow sucking it up and sticking to the retreat schedule? Or would I open up as a fellow traveler in need of deep emotional healing? At that moment, I could hide behind my professional title and position, or I could enter into the journey and risk rejection.

It was a dangerous call. In seminary, I'd been instructed to not be vulnerable. Under no circumstance were pastors supposed to let their emotions get out of control. Your support system was supposed to be other pastors in the community and people outside of your congregation. You weren't supposed to break down in the pulpit or expose your weak, frail reality. And although they'd never said it, I was pretty sure the same rules applied for a weekend retreat.

In many ways, the strategies I learned as a tram driver in Sacramento were the same ones preached by my professors in seminary. Keep it moving. Stay on track. Follow the script. Don't deviate from the route. Don't get too close to people. These were the keys to a bright, secure future. Bawling like a baby definitely was not on the itinerary.

Still, I felt the Spirit calling me to something more that day—something other than business as usual. It was as if I could hear the Spirit saying, "You need to come clean. You need to be honest. I'm giving you an opportunity to come out of hiding."

Reluctantly, I got up and blurted out, "That's me! I am that man...and I hope I can find the courage to learn this lesson and see what forgiveness and freedom is all about." It didn't take long for my words to turn into sobbing and then all-out blubbering. My soul was wailing so deeply within me I could hardly stand. Forget the schedule. Forget the agenda. I had now entered uncharted territory.

Looking back, I see that event as one where I crossed the line from tour guide to fellow traveler. As a pastor, I had been trained to run retreats and to run them well. As a teaching pastor, I knew the importance of having the right answer and presenting my message in a concise, media-savvy way. My job was to know the way and to tell people exactly what to do to know God. Three points and a poem—that's what I was trained to do.

For centuries, the tour guide metaphor has dominated our religious experience. We've defined evangelism and spiritual leadership in terms of a hierarchical relationship: one person finds the way and tells someone else how to get there. By contrast, the church of the future—the emerging church—would seem to embrace a more collaborative leadership model. The metaphor is that of a traveler—someone who is "on the way," journeying with us. They still may have more experience and expertise than we do, but they don't need the security of their position/title. They can lead a group without having to know absolutely everything about the final destination.

Pastors who have adopted the traveler metaphor don't necessarily break down in tears each Sunday, but they do acknowledge their weaknesses and vulnerabilities. They understand that everyone has something to contribute, and they aren't afraid to admit when they don't have all the answers.

As a culture, we've long since abandoned the idea of perfect leaders and perfect plans. When we see individuals and ideas presented in neat, airbrushed packages, we're cynical. We know both have faults and we resent any attempt to pretend otherwise. The church, however, has been reluctant to admit this reality. Despite all our talk of sin and needing a Savior, we insist on looking like the exception. By fixing our attention on tightly worded tracts, well-executed programs, and other people's problems, we avoid having to see ourselves as we really are. People attending church today, however, have little patience for this kind of sanctified denial. Instead, we hunger for a place where honesty and authenticity are embraced. We can see their appetite on sites like TheOoze.com.

At times, TheOoze message boards have been criticized for being a hotbed of negativity—a bunch of people whining about the church. As you listen in on the following conversations, however, I think you'll begin to see that what seems like rant is, in fact, often a passionate cry for a new guiding metaphor—in this case, a desire to see tour guides become travelers.

Topic: Postmodern Leadership?

[Posted by: suppliants]

What follows is my first rant here at TheOoze:

Leadership, schmedership. Why are Christians so obsessed with leadership? Everyone wants to be a chief...and no one wants to be an Indian. Just go to any Christian bookstore. There are piles of

---

books on the topic of leadership. There's even a leadership Bible!
Whatever happened to followership, servanthood, the greatest being
the least, etc.?

Or better yet, why doesn't someone write a book about Jesus'
effective leadership secrets—like when many of his followers were
deserting him and the disciples were worried and Jesus turns and
says, "Unless you eat the flesh of the Son of Man and drink his
blood, you have no life in you" (John 6:53). Hey, pastors, try that
the next time people are thinking about exiting your church. Or
how about spitting in the dirt and rubbing it in a blind man's
eyes? Or going into a Christian bookstore and knocking over the
shelves? Or calling a minority a "dog"? How about NOT organizing a
meeting, teleconference, 3-point sermon, Website, BLOG, Bible study,
how-to book, etc., and instead hanging out at the pub with your
mates? Or go and eat at the house of the town's most flamboy-
ant homosexual couple? Yep, that'll really get you far in today's
evangelical leadership-obsessed church culture (far out the door!).

Yes, I know we need leadership in the church. I got that. My
problem is the model of leadership I have personally seen. It is
more based on controlling others and propping up the ridiculous
insecurities of the so-called leaders than actually serving others
and building them up in Christ. Yes, there are many humble,
Christ-like leaders in the Body...these I am NOT referring to in
this, my first of all rants.

[Posted by: preachinjesus]

As I look through leadership down through the ages, it appears to
me that although our methods might change, several factors will
remain the same:

1. Leadership, to be effective, must be relational at its base
   (this is true now more than ever).
2. Your vision must be fresh and refreshed constantly.
3. Your followers love stories.
4. Leadership rises and falls on one's abilities and example.
5. Leadership does have a requirement of Providence to be
   truly effective.
6. Leadership must be servant-centered (i.e. the leader
   must serve primarily).

[Posted by: footer]

Let's see...leadership. Hmmmmm...here are some steps to effective leadership:
◦Be a chicken and thresh wheat in a winepress while waiting for a
  celestial being to tell you what to do.

- Build a giant boat—and make sure to get silly drunk afterward.
- Spend 40 years watching your father-in-law's sheep...you probably
  won't really be ready for leadership until you're at least 80.
  Some kind of mystical experience with a glowing plant might help, too.
- Kill a giant.
- Be as obnoxious as possible...you know, go around naked for three
  years, sleep by a fire of dung, wear some type of bondage
  device and declare it has spiritual significance.
- Run from positions of leadership—like being made king—as often
  as possible.
- Be executed by the government.

These are just some examples I have found.

[Posted by: footer]

Now, on a more serious note...

It seems to me that the current focus by the church on the
whole leadership thing is fairly new—perhaps conceived in the
Industrial Age and being birthed more fully now. I think it comes
out of that American success ethic version of Christianity.
Historically, we would do well to simply focus on things like
integrity, sacrifice, and the mysterious voice of God. While the
current leadership-talk mentions these things, it tends to lead
more strongly toward issues of style, hype, and the ability to
manipulate and politic. Just like success, God doesn't seem to place
much emphasis on leadership...faithfulness seems to be the key.

Some people use sarcasm and others shoot straight, but the message is the same: we need a new leadership paradigm. Our present model doesn't seem to have much in common with Scripture. It doesn't match Jesus Christ or any other biblical "great." In these posts, you hear the call to move away from a secular business model and instead find something that more closely matches Jesus Christ's example.

[Posted by: suppliants]

When I look through the Bible and see the type of people God
tends to use (liars, cheats, wimps, runts, etc.), I am always both
perplexed and encouraged. Perplexed because it makes no sense in
the natural scheme of things (Why was David, the runt, chosen
when all his brothers seemed much more qualified?), and encouraged
because I am also a liar, cheat, wimp, runt, etc.

[Posted by: angie]

I hate to be one of the ones to disagree and not hop on the "I
hate leadership" beer truck, but...

The Bible does talk about leadership. It just doesn't talk about perfect leaders or slick, fake leaders. It talks about LEADERS like we think of leadership. I think there is so much negative connotation to those words, "leader, leadership," yet it doesn't make the idea ineffectual.

1 Timothy 4:12 (NLT)—"Don't let anyone think less of you because you are young. Be an example to all believers in what you teach, in the way you live, in your love, your faith, and your purity."

If that's not leadership, I don't know what is. Webster says:
"The position or office of a leader;
Capacity or ability to lead;
A group of leaders;
Guidance; direction."

If we don't think there's a facet of true leadership development within leading the church, be it postmodern or not, we're fooling ourselves.

Here we see the counter argument—the "What are you really saying?" post. Does becoming a traveler mean sitting back and being passive? Does it mean no one gives any guidance or direction? How far are we willing to go to fix what ails us? In an effort to reform the church, will we swing too hard in the opposite direction?

[Posted by: frankenberry]

No one is saying they hate leadership. What we are saying is that the concept has been distorted in the modern church into something that looks more like the world than the kingdom of God.

Look at the example you pointed out. BE AN EXAMPLE. Paul is encouraging Timothy to be a leader by displaying the love, the life, and the mind of Christ to others. You're right, that is a true Acts 2 church leader. Paul didn't tell Timothy to study theology and leadership for 3 years. He didn't tell him to start calling himself "Reverend" or "Head Pastor" or "Executive Minister in Charge of Discipline and Growth" for God's sake. He didn't tell him to go write a book on the subject or start on the lecture circuit. He told him to go show it. Be a servant. Wasn't that a catchy phrase for a while—"servant leader"?

If you want to be first (i.e., a leader) in the kingdom of God, you must first make yourself a servant of the world. Not the sort that distorts that verse into something manipulative telling people how to live their lives. But simply loving people. You don't need a title or position or "worldly authority" or a top-down, hierarchical institution to do that. Indeed, those things probably do more to hinder someone from true leadership.

One of the great things about TheOoze is the dialogue that happens between people. I'm always inspired when I see how positive the discussion can be, even when opinions differ. "Flaming" seems to be a rarity. What's more, everyone on TheOoze is an equal. There are no titles, roles, or positions. In that sense, it really is a group of travelers journeying together.

Topic: Qualifications for Leadership

[Posted by: robbay828]

I am on a committee looking to hire a new senior pastor.. There is a candidate that I am personally extremely drawn to. He appears to have all the skills necessary for the position: equipping others to do ministry, strategic planning and visioning, leadership development, etc. He also has a deep passion for evangelism and seems to have a real grasp of ministering to people of our wounded and broken generation. My concern is that he gained his transparency, vulnerability, and sensitivity as a result of completely crashing his life. Even in this anonymous forum, I want to be careful to protect his story, but trust me to say that he took the leap off the high dive of rational behavior and crashed hard at the bottom of the pool. All of this happened during a leave of absence from active full-time ministry. After several years of therapy and God's transforming power of forgiveness and healing, he again feels the call of full-time ministry.

One of the issues I struggle with is how broken is too broken. I know that Galatians 6 calls us to restore our broken family members fully and gently, but I balance that with the idea that leaders are called to a higher standard. It would seem to me that in this day and age, brokenness is just a regular part of life. Everyone I know has dealt with fairly substantial issues. One of the blessings of this age seems to be that we are more open to talk about those issues and work on the healing process within community. I think this person's story of healing and restoration to Christ...to his family...to the Body could have tremendous impact on our community. I also fear that those who would not see the benefit of this story might destroy his ability to minister effectively among us. What insight can you share? What are the qualifications for leadership within this culture? Don't they change along with everything else, or are they timeless?

[Posted by: sharont7]

I have thought about this question a lot over the past couple of years. I think the conclusion I have come to is that I have so much respect for leaders who have gone through much crap in life and still come out on the other side with passion for God—a desire to serve him and others no matter what. If this guy has gone through a very hard time and yet still shows so much fruit, he sounds like an excellent leader. I have seen many "leaders" criticize leaders who have fallen. They lack grace and understanding of where this person is coming from. A lot of times people are so quick to judge a person's past, they fail to look at the fruit that he/she is displaying now. Yes, I believe that when you are looking at someone to fill a staff role, you should look at the whole picture, but my philosophy has always been that current fruit should take higher priority than the past. In the crap of life, when everything seems to hit rock bottom, I believe those are the times that God can strip everything away and refine us with his fire into who he desires us to be.

Here are some great "rubber meets the road" posts. How willing are we to embrace brokenness in our leaders? How broken is too broken? How many leaders in the Bible would actually live up to our contemporary expectations for leadership? And if we encourage leaders to hang up their microphones and journey along beside us, are we ready to stand by them in that experience? How can we allow our leaders to be real, honest, and authentic without compromising the health of the church?

Topic: Leadership in the emerging church?

[Posted by: Polycarp]

My observation is that we borrow leadership models that work from the broader culture. For example, after World War II most leadership models were military. Leaders were distant, non-relational, tough decision-makers.

After the great wars, the big task at hand was to advance the quality of life. A new model emerged because of the success of leaders like Steven Jobs, Bill Gates, Michael Eisner, etc. I call them missional leaders—people who rally and organize everyone in your organization around the mission. If you listened to people at Apple in the early years (and even now), you would think you were at a church conference. Church leadership borrowed (and was borrowed from) to develop the current celebrated style of leaders—the leader as keeper of the mission. Mission is king!

The postmodern world is rejecting mission as arbitrary. I think the new leadership model is a simple model. A leader is simply a compelling person. Strong relationally. Not sacrificing relationships for the sake of mission. Honest, not over-promising. Able to hold a diverse group of people together without marginalizing people. Making decisions and keeping the mission are pieces of cake compared to developing and maintaining relationships.

[Posted by: mr_magoo]

Wow, mind expansion is painful....

Nice description of a leader in these changing times, Polycarp.

Are there figures in the broader culture that model this type of leadership?

[Posted by: Polycarp]

think the business world is going through a major redefinition of leadership. In today's world, everyone is "self-employed." You might agree to work for a company for compensation, but your ideas are not the property of that company unless you can obtain some form of "ownership" that will reward your ideas. If you cannot obtain some form of ownership, you probably will leave that company to explore opportunities for your ideas elsewhere. What I find so interesting is that our parents had a work ethic that said "stay loyal to your company." A "good resume" was one job for a long time. Today's "good resume" has a collection of companies and work experiences.

Who are the leaders of the new workers today? The people with compensation who can be exchanged for the performance of a task? I don't think so. I think the new leaders are people who you want to share life with. I think these new models are just emerging. I think the business world is stuck right now. I think the new leadership models may actually emerge from the church, and we will teach the broader culture how to lead and organize again.

We are in the midst of transition. While we've come to realize that our present image of leadership is faulted, finding a suitable replacement is hard work. Honesty is hard work. Consequently, there are times when we may be tempted to return to where we've been. Perhaps we'll see a John Wayne movie and think, "Yeah, that's what leadership should be! Enough of this touchy-feely stuff. We need to get things done." Yet the reality is that returning to the leadership models of the past will not help move the church forward. As Polycarp suggests, we have a great opportunity in front of us. We not only have a chance to determine what our leadership model will be, but we also can share that model with the wider culture.

[Posted by: JAK]

I know this is going to sound heretical, but maybe we are placing too much emphasis on leaders in the church. Somehow it reminds me of those thunder boys, James & John, trying to figure out who would be the big kahunas.

I may be naive or idealistic, but I've yet to see the body of Christ gather with any kind of consistency when the Lord didn't start emerging through various individuals (Romans 12). Teachers start to teach, leaders lead, givers give...you get the picture. Seems to me that's how the early church did a lot of their "church organizing." They observed and confirmed God in people.

To me, that is organic life, not some kind of test tube, mechanical formula church. Just add marketing, build a building, throw in a zillion programs—oh, and a whole lot of money—and you got church.

Oh, did I forget the people? OOPS. Seems a lot of church leaders forget the sheep they are called to care for, too!

[Posted by: moshie]

---QUOTED---
I may be naive or idealistic, but I've yet to see the body of Christ gather with any kind of consistency when the Lord didn't start emerging through various individuals.
---END QUOTE---

I love your perspective—it sounds a lot like the people Jesus Christ prayed for in Matthew 11:25—26, "Abruptly Jesus broke into prayer: 'Thank you, Father, Lord of heaven and earth. You've concealed your ways from sophisticates and know-it-alls, but spelled them out clearly to ordinary people. Yes, Father, that's the way you like to work'" [THE MESSAGE].

It excites me to be with a group of people journeying together as a community, taking equal responsibility. Jesus shining through them. Please pray for me, bro, I'm in a community that's part of a megachurch. My role there: being subversive. The test tube, mechanical church drives me nuts. Some days I just want to throw tables over like our Mentor.

The transition from tour guide to traveler is difficult. Changing the picture in our heads is one thing; beginning to move toward it is quite another. When it comes right down to it, giving up our identity as tour guides requires one thing: courage. Looking back, so much of my life has been about trying to duplicate someone else's program. Why? Because I wanted to do life "right." I wanted to succeed in ministry.

I've come to see that fear motivates tour guides. Spiritual tour guides zealously try to control life to ensure they will be valued. They constantly fear that their last achievement will not be enough to cover them today. From far away, they may look confident and competent, but inside they tremble with anxiety. Their sense of worth inevitably comes from their position of authority and performing their duties well.

In my own life, I'm beginning to understand that I will never feel secure as long as I am duplicating other people's programs—whether it's an evangelism strategy or a particular approach to quiet times. You know what? All my life I've struggled with quiet times. It's not that I haven't worked at it, but that I've worked too hard. By trying to follow someone else's model, I turned quiet times into busy times. I would arm myself with highlighters and notebooks, reference books and workbooks. Like a kid with too much homework, I resented the time I spent and yet at the same time drew a sense of worth from completing a lesson. The day I found the courage to unplug the quiet time machine and instead truly rest in God's presence, my world changed.

I've discovered I don't have to sharpen my Number 2 pencil and vigorously fill in the blanks to grow in my relationship with God. I don't have to read the Bible in a year or complete some kind of intensive Scripture memorization program. I can meditate on just one verse of Scripture, one word even. I can go for walks, sit silently, and just listen—all without an agenda.

Tour guides don't feel free to deviate from the "route" other Christians have set. What's more, they're apt to impose that same kind of rigid structure on others. Becoming a traveler, however, enables you to be true to yourself. When you're not feeding on the approval of others, you're free to wander off the beaten path and rest when you need to. As a result, you begin to hear from God along the entire journey, not just at the destination or pre-determined photo ops.

Then there's the issue of what I call "stickiness." When I'm guided by the image of a traveler, people can come near me without feeling I will take something from them. I can hug people without needing them to hug back. In youth ministry, we used to have a saying: "Never take a hug." The fact is, looking for assurance from those you have authority over, and orchestrating circumstances to extract that approval, is wrong.

As a traveler, I am free to love and be loved. I'm not worried about taking a wrong-step or losing my position. I'm just one more person on the journey—a beloved child of God. I don't have to do anything to be accepted. I'm loved exactly as I am. My sense of worth and rightness come from Jesus Christ.

Does being a traveler mean I never take the initiative with a group? Not at all. But it means I don't have to sit behind the wheel all the time.

Application

1. Where are you on the continuum between tour guide and traveler?

Tour Guide	Traveler
• I know the "right" and "best" ways	• I'm on the journey
• I'm an expert with a reputation to uphold	• I'm learning from you
• My job is to tell you exactly what to do	• I'm open to finding new ways to do things
• Believes "I must know the right answer"	• "I don't have to have it all figured out"

2. What keeps you from journeying alongside people?

3. What risk(s) do you think you might have to take to become more of a traveler?

TEACHER
TO
Facilitator

A Conversation about "Learning"

CHAPTER **3**

I love the Psalms. I love the raw emotion that gushes out as David and others confess their inadequacies, cry out for mercy, and long to see justice come down on their enemies. For some reason, the Psalms touch me in a way that other books of the Bible do not.

The opposite of Psalms is Romans. In that rather formal letter, Paul carefully lays out the foundations of the Christian faith by following a specific order and pattern of logic. I imagine him agonizing over each word of the letter, struggling to get every nuance just right according to the prompting of the Holy Spirit.

By comparison, the Psalms seem earthy and spontaneous. Equally inspired, the words strike me as less edited, less contrived.

A few years back, I decided I wanted to remind people at my church that they could be real with God and encourage them not to suppress their emotions (as if suppressing them were somehow more "spiritual"). As I set about preparing the lesson, I became more and more convinced that just teaching on the subject wasn't going to cut it. I needed to engage people, to somehow create an environment where they could interact with the Psalms in a fresh way.

I decided to dole out clay. Lots of it. The idea was pretty straightforward. I simply asked the congregation to track with me as I talked—to sculpt emotions as I read through various Psalms. Occasionally, I'd ask them to make audible sounds matching those emotions. I still remember looking out and seeing 700 people growling and holding up little spiky sculptures while I talked about anger.

Playing with clay in a church service may seem silly, but it was a powerful way of getting people in touch with their feelings. Even more powerful was the time of communion at the end of the service. Earlier in the service, I had asked each person to make a sculpture depicting the emotion he or she felt most at that particular moment. In preparation for the table, I asked them to stand up and bring their sculptures to the cross, naming the emotion as they came. Artist Doug Tennapel watched this procession carefully from the sidelines and then set about turning the hundreds of individual sculptures into one large creation.

When communion was over, I asked Doug to explain his creation to the congregation. For the next few minutes, he shared about his experiences. He talked about what he had observed—and why he felt compelled to form a lamb being destroyed by a serpent and the serpent being overtaken by a lion.

Those few minutes were invaluable. There was no doubt in my mind that Doug was exactly where God wanted him to be. He was using his gift to encourage the rest of the congregation. He wasn't just an add-on to the service (or a sideshow in the foyer). Instead, he was an integral part of the worship event. He was doing something I never could have done.

Looking back, I see myself not so much as a teacher, but as a facilitator. Unlike most other Sundays, my role that week wasn't to dispense information or even give a particularly thought-provoking sermon. Instead, it was to encourage people in their own learning—to create an environment where they could discover God for themselves.

The shift

As I think about the emerging church, I see a similar shift occurring. In most traditional churches, the pastor's role is to teach. As the fount of all knowledge, the pastor's job is to overflow with spiritual truth each week while the congregation sits and absorbs this wisdom. Sure, there are other elements in a service—like music and prayer—but for the most part, the sermon is the focal point.

With so much riding on the weekly message, churches are susceptible to "charismatic" leaders—for better or for worse. Each Sunday, the pastor must deliver something new and inspirational to the congregation, lest he or she become the topic of conversation at lunch. As the name on the marquee outside, the pastor is inextricably linked to the success or failure of the church.

In many ways, the modern worship service is a thinly disguised university lecture. Congregants file in, face the front and frantically take notes while an established scholar—a spiritual giant in their midst—passes on formulas for a more fulfilling life.

At some churches, of course, the environment feels less academic and more like a TV show, complete with frequent applause from the audience. Theatre-style seating, stage lights, and video projectors often complete the effect. Part business presentation, part talk show, the modern "seeker-sensitive" service aims to entertain as well as educate. Engagement with all five senses is optional.

Church wasn't always this way, of course. Go back several centuries and worship was a decidedly sensual experience. Your sense of awe inevitably began on the ride into town. Looking up, you'd see the church spire on the horizon, then the sharply pitched roof and the colorful stained glass windows. Enter through the massive wooden doors and you'd be greeted with the sweet smell of incense—a scent so distinct, you'd recognize it anywhere. Often you'd place your knee on a cold, hard floor and dip your hand into a bowl of cool, refreshing water.

Upon completing these rituals you'd take your place on a hand-carved bench, perhaps one crafted by an uncle or grandfather. Sitting there in the stillness, you couldn't help but be reminded of the awesomeness of God. A few moments later, the procession would come down the aisle and your eyes would struggle to take it all in—the colorful vestments, the swinging censor, the golden cross.

From behind you, the high-pitched sounds of a choir would ring out, their angelic praise reverberating off the rough-hewn walls. Then there was the celebration of the Eucharist, the reciting of prayers, and other rituals. Every element was carefully planned and executed for dramatic effect. It seemed God was "wholly other," far greater than we could ever comprehend, and thus worthy of much pageantry. Church engaged all your senses and worship was a full-bodied affair. Priests were present, but hardly the stars of the show—especially since they rarely used the language of the people.

But times changed, of course. People grew tired of all the ritual. Church leaders abused their power and symbols lost their meaning. As the Enlightenment took hold, worship became a much more rational endeavor. Soon every element was about engaging the mind and presenting a logical, well-reasoned argument. In time, sanctuaries began to look like classrooms and pastors began looking more and more like college professors.

Somehow, over the centuries, knowledge has become king. We've effectively said that knowing about God will ultimately help us know God. As a result, we often focused more on the Word, than on the Word become flesh. And yet, as A.W. Tozer pointed out, God cannot be contained in any object or that object will become our god. Could it be that we've created an idol and have actually begun to worship Christian education or the Bible?

Churches today have been expressly designed for passing on knowledge. Objects that appeal to the senses have been removed. Ironically, this switch to a "user-friendly" environment is problematic for many postmodern people—the very people churches say they want to reach. While there is something to be said for comfortable chairs and trouble-free parking, slick worship services seem exactly that—slick. It's Amway with a thin spiritual veneer.

Thom S. Rainer, dean of the Billy Graham School of Missions, Evangelism, and Church Growth at Southern Baptist Seminary in Louisville, Kentucky, told The Washington Times that the main reason people leave church is it's too similar to their everyday lives. Could it be the seeker-sensitive movement has actually backfired?

Another way

People seem to be hungering for a return to mysticism. Increasingly, they want to encounter the Divine, not just hear a great sermon. They want to experience God sensually, not just understand cognitively.

Consider the renewed interest in rituals. Practices that were once seen as dry and dusty are now embraced as fresh expressions of faith and opportunities to tap into the rich heritage of our Christian ancestors. At the same time, however, postmodern people are also eager to try new things—to break away from tradition and encounter Jesus Christ in their own unique, uncensored ways.

Postmodern people don't want to be preached at so much as encouraged. Whereas teachers impart information, facilitators create opportunities for learning. They understand the importance of experience-based learning. They're not afraid to invite others to participate in the learning journey and to take over on occasion, adding their unique perspective to the mix. And they're not concerned with reputation in quite the same way. Since facilitators are not the "stars" of the church, but rather the individuals who keep things moving, they often feel less pressure to perform. They're free to try new things, to experiment, and to let the Holy Spirit truly lead.

In all this, I can't help but think of Jesus. Yes, he taught on occasion, but he also spent a lot of time just being with people. He created opportunities for individuals to discover on their own what his kingdom was about. He used stories, metaphors, and parables to speak into people's lives. And Jesus didn't simply teach—he often healed people, fed or ate with them, traveled together by boat, and leisurely walked with them along the road.

We often say that Jesus is the greatest teacher of all, but in actual fact, the Scriptures show Jesus formally teaching only a few times. The rest of the accounts describe him helping people learn in the context of their real lives—coming alongside them, asking thought-provoking questions, and giving them an opportunity to fit the pieces together on their own.

The idea of worship—what it should and shouldn't be—is a hot topic in the emerging church. But at the root of that conversation are often deeper questions about pastoral leadership. Just what is the role of the pastor? Have we become so enamored with teaching that we've actually inhibited spiritual growth?

Topic: Leadership in the emerging church?

[Posted by: moshie]

The last few months I've been part of a team that meets as a leadership for our community. We share a meal together and chat about what God is doing in our lives. Lately I'm wondering what the leadership structure of the emerging culture would look like. One of my conclusions is that the modern church placed huge emphasis on the gift of leadership and spent a huge amount of time defining that gift through a CEO/Stephen Covey, et al., lens. This effectively squashed all the other gifts and what we can bring to the party. I believe that we should have a balanced view of leadership shepherding leaders, teaching leaders, apostolic leaders, messed up leaders.... NO ONE-MAN SHOWS.

[Posted by: adcreech]

Our big challenge regarding leadership in the emerging church is going to be letting go of control, but not giving up the idea of leadership all together. Many have just jettisoned the idea no leadership. Nope. Others have put far too much emphasis on "the dude" as the only conduit through which God can build or strengthen the church. Nope. Getting our balance will be difficult.

[Posted by: jmyers]

I am not convinced that we lead people. People lead themselves.

What I observe when someone has leading gifts is they are gifted in helping others lead their own lives forward. The definition of leading has become a little skewed. It has almost nothing to do with controlling, fixing, knowing what's best, and other commonly held views.

It is freeing to know that Jesus promoted helping others with their lives as leading. For him, giving almost enough help to be helpful was leading. I don't have to know what is best for others. I don't have to fix their life. I provide them help and they lead their own life.

[Posted by: moshie]

---QUOTED---
It has almost nothing to do with controlling, fixing, knowing what's best, and other commonly held views.
---END QUOTE---

Leadership should be a natural outflow of a community walking together—where the best course of action is a product of the

> "Aha!" moments of the community. The leader is the person who has
> the ability to frame the "Aha!" moment. People inspire and infuse
> each other. Thus all the "one another" admonitions in the Bible. The
> challenge is to get away from the model where one person con-
> stantly creates the "Aha!" moment—because it always leads to some
> kind of manipulation. And over time resembles more of a fart than
> a fragrance. Does this make sense?

Do sermons stink? No, really, I mean it. How valuable is the traditional sermon? What value does it add to people's lives? Is it the best way of communicating God's truth—or is it more like a bad infomercial?

> [Posted by: tammy]
>
> ---QUOTED---
> People lead themselves.
> ---END QUOTE---
>
> How does that jive with the Scriptures where Jesus looks at the
> people without leadership and mourns, because they wander around
> like lost sheep?
>
> I think of most people as followers. Few of us have original ideas
> about anything.
>
> [Posted by: jmyers]
>
> I think we need to take a clean look at "shepherd."
>
> Shepherds do not lead sheep. There is an understanding between
> sheep and shepherd. Sheep lead their own lives forward. Shepherds
> help sheep with their lives. They marshal, drive, guide, steer, pro-
> pel, and direct. These activities are hardly ever performed from
> the front.
>
> These words are great synonyms for leader. However, in each of
> these words there is a recognition that you are not truly in con-
> trol. You are in agreement.

For professional clergy, the stakes are particularly high. Are we willing to risk los-ing our identity for the sake of Jesus Christ?

Again, we see people willing to ask the tough questions. What does it mean to "shepherd" a church? Language, remember, is not an exact science, and so part of the unpackaging process involves taking a fresh look at our terms. Shepherds are a great example. In explaining the Christmas story, I've often heard pastors describe the shepherds as "the kind of guys you wouldn't let date your daughter," and yet Jesus calls himself "the good shepherd." What does the word "shepherd" imply? Is the shepherd the definitive model for biblical leadership?

[Posted by: moshie]

I think this might be one of the strengths of emerging leadership. We should be conduits, helping others to be drawn to God, not ourselves. Background leadership will be as, if not more, important than "stage" leadership. First Corinthians 3:7 says, "So neither he who plants nor he who waters is anything, but only God, who makes things grow."

Some of the most influential people in my life were background/ordinary people. They pointed me to God.

Topic: a new kind of pastor

[Posted by: footer]

...The truth is that when I was in professional ministry I liked to be in charge. I liked to make things happen. I liked being "successful." I liked being told I was doing great. I liked hearing through the grapevine that people talked about what we were doing with a sense of awe. I liked being considered an expert. I liked being offered jobs and getting raises because of it. I liked building my own little comfortable kingdom...until I realized how empty it was. Maybe part of the issue really has been, is, and will be us. Maybe we've created all these expectations congregations have.

We need to be willing to take a closer look at our own hearts when it comes to leadership. The reality is, pastors do get something out of being pastors. The problem, I think, is many of us aren't willing to admit it. We're fearful of what we might find.

[Posted by: ezekiel]

PREACH-O-MATIC

New! Improved! With features that include a fresh stylish leisure suit, impeccable hair, a Rolex watch with a compass pointing to the nearest restaurant, and a special "sermon setting" for 30 minutes, 45 minutes, or a special three-hour option for those who just can't get enough of that good, good stuff.

Available in navy, turquoise, avocado green, and of course, black.

```
If you act now, we'll also send you "The Boxing Nun"™.
It's great for a Denominational Death Match.

Call now. Operators are standing by.
```

The story is told about Ghandi meeting E. Stanley Jones. When Jones asked Ghandi about his spiritual beliefs, he reportedly said, in essence, "Oh, I don't reject your Christ. I love your Christ. It's just that so many of you Christians are so unlike your Christ." Again, we need to be willing to see ourselves as others see us—no matter how much it hurts.

```
Topic: jazz preaching

Started: Wednesday December 11, 2002 6:22 PM


[Posted by: mr_magoo]

Here's my stupid idea I'd like to try someday. Anyone seen anything
like this?

Pick a topic and four people of varying backgrounds.
The four get together a couple of times to drink coffee and talk
about the topic.

On Sunday morning, they do that again, only in front of people.

You get the improvisation of a jazz quartet, where each player
knows what the other one will do, supporting the other in order to
create something. It is like a panel discussion except the point isn't
to win an argument, but to make something beautiful together.


[Posted by: preachinjesus]

Isn't "jazz preaching" (i.e. improv preaching) what Primitive Baptists
do every Sunday?


[Posted by: tammy]

Primitive Baptists. I'm showing my prejudice, but I think of people
trying to outdo each other.

The quartet—sounds more like a cooperative effort, with no lone
ranger heroes.
```

[Posted by: the_soulsurfer]

I've always been intrigued by Paul's instructions to the Corinthians about their gatherings.... Remember where he said that two or three prophets should speak and everyone weigh out what they say. If a revelation comes to someone sitting down, the first should stop.... It's a give and take sort of thing so that "everyone is instructed." That has always seemed to me like what Magoo is describing...a sort of improv. I suppose that's what PJ is saying about the Primitive Baptists...but there is such a cacophony in that, it seems hard to be instructed. I had always experimented more with interactive discussion (timed things, approaches inspired by Fight Club...), but I really like the idea of a limited number of speakers, with a pre-arranged agenda, and then a spontaneous weaving of perspective and idea around the subject.

[Posted by: robbay828]

Many years ago I was attending a church where one week the associate pastor sat amongst the congregation and during the senior pastor's sermon, stood up and asked some really good questions. They dialogued for about five to 10 minutes, then the senior pastor continued. All the senior pastor knew ahead of time was that he might be interrupted. It was a huge success. People really responded to hearing the questions that were bouncing around in their head articulated and discussed. Future attempts to capture the spontaneity didn't work as well, but I thought the exchanges were awesome!

[Posted by: angie]

I personally would love to take part in something like that. Conversation rather than talking head...I like it.

Finding the right balance between talking heads and unstructured chaos isn't easy. Just the same, I think we owe it to ourselves to start trying new things—new ways of interacting with each other and the Word as part of "worship."

The danger, of course, will be latching onto something new that "works" and exchanging one formula for another. Today's drama could easily become tomorrow's sermon.

Topic: Consumerism or Paganism

[Posted by: footer]

I wonder what it would be like if a preacher did nothing but quote the words of Jesus Christ for a few weeks in a sermon. How would the congregation respond?

It's an interesting point, but others are saying, in effect, "Look, it isn't what's being said in the sermon that's the problem. The sermon itself is the problem." That seems to be a common sentiment in the emerging church. Again, people are beginning to question whether the most effective way to develop disciples is by teaching in a lecture format.

[Posted by: TheMuse]

Don't you think church would be more eventful if you let some of the onlookers teach or sing a hymn or something? Why do you think people transmigrate from churches so much? There's no practical involvement to bring about change in their lives. People need to exercise the information they've been storing away. How can they when their only function is to sit and watch?

[Posted by: tammy]

My husband spent nearly a year reading through the Bible, chapter by chapter, aloud to the congregation, and commenting on what he was reading. Not that he didn't prepare (he did read it at home beforehand and do some study), but he didn't make any notes. He just spoke to what he felt God was trying to say to us on that day through that Scripture. He covered several books of the Bible this way. Some people loved it. A few accused him of not "preaching the Word." (What ELSE was he reading, then??) Most didn't seem to notice that much had changed!

[Posted by: TheMuse]

You know what I've always wanted to do:

You know that part in a preacher's sermon when he says, "Is anyone getting this?" I wanna jump up and say, "Yeah, I got it and you know what else? I think this could be applied to this, this and this...."

I'm sorry, but it gets really old being on the end of a one-way conversation. Why even ask the congregation? Are they just looking for an "Amen" to feel good about themselves? Or are they really trying to teach me? This is why so many teens are getting lost. Their minds are going 180 mph and they can't even give feedback.

AAAAAArgh!!! What can be done????

What portion of a worship service needs to be about teaching to make it a valid event? What becomes of the senior pastor if he preaches less and the congregation participates more? In the megachurch, the senior pastor has already offloaded all the traditional pastoral care responsibilities to others. He's the CEO, not the one who visits hospitals and prisons. If he stops preaching, what then?

> [Posted by: dwight]
>
> Our homily is very much akin to speeches in the Roman Court. Jesus had a more Socratic method of teaching that was highly interactive. Plenty of feedback. I have a friend, God bless him, he's not all there, but he will stop a pastor in the middle of a sermon to ask for clarification. The church isn't large, and no one seems to mind.

Somehow we've made knowledge the zenith of the Christian life. And yet, how many Bible verses and stories does the average Christian know? How much is all that knowledge making an impact for the kingdom? The challenge of the emerging church is to wrestle through these questions—to take a hard look at the aggressive educational system we've cloaked as worship and then risk suggesting other ways. Alternative worship may be a part of the answer.

Topic: Alternative Worship

> [Posted by: kirstin]
>
> In a church I attend, we are working on starting a service that would incorporate alternative worship styles in more than just music. We are talking about different ways of having communion together, different ways of speaking/sharing, the possibility of foot washing and of group serving. Do you have thoughts or suggestions for alternative styles of worship? I would love to hear them and pass them on to the pastor I am working with.

One of the characteristics of the emerging church is a willingness to make worship a less stage-driven activity. I think it's fair to say that worship is being decentralized. People are being released to worship in their own unique ways.

> [Posted by: aaronsharem]
>
> I took our home group through a worship experience where I gave each person a picture to meditate on and then pray about.
>
> I have also played a song about heaven by MercyMe called "I Can Only Imagine," then had each person draw a picture of themselves meeting Jesus or describe how they imagine the experience.
>
> [Posted by: sudrumguy]
>
> We have a thing called the four corners. During the singing/musical time, people are heartily encouraged, if they feel led, to "visit a corner."

In one corner, there are some stones, a bucket of water, and some other containers filled with sand. The stones represent things we need to let go of and are dropped in the water. A person is encouraged to write their sins in the sand and then wipe them away as symbolic of what Jesus Christ has already done for us.

In another corner is a prayer area, where a person can light a candle as they pray for someone else. These candles then melt together on a large platter, indicating all the prayers that have gone to God.

Another area is devoted to "artistic" or "creative" worship. We have different things artists can use (large canvas, paint, pencils, notebook paper).... This is also the area where people can give money or time or drop their information card.

The last corner is the Lord's Supper, communion—whatever you like to call it...

[Posted by: nilomeca]

Yeah, I've experienced a few alternative worship elements. One was writing poetry, another was being creative with clay and paint, and another was a sort of candle lighting....

[Posted by: jmorgan]

Howdy!

I had a chance to worship with Bobby from Coast Hills Church in Southern California this last year. During one of the songs, he had a series of images of Jesus Christ through different paintings, both new and old. I forget how many there were, maybe 20? But as these images were flashing on the screen, we were also walking to the cross to take communion. It was really intense....

[Posted by: Butterfly]

My husband and I started and hosted a worship circle 1x/month. We would lay out all kinds of acoustic instruments (guitars, hand drums, tambourines, blocks, bells, tin whistle, etc.) and other things that made sound for anyone to take during our time of prayer and worship. It was very open, with no specific worship or prayer leader. At one time a girl brought artwork to share. It...really challenged us to trust each other more and we grew closer because of it. More importantly, we came to rely more on the Holy Spirit's leading.

While all these ideas are great, I think it's important not to slip into an "Ohhh...so that's what postmodern worship is!" mindset. These posts describe expressions of worship that worked for specific communities. The "what" in worship isn't nearly as important as the "how." It's the authenticity that matters and whether the expression matches the worshiper's heart. Doing something different just to be different—or doing it because it's cool—isn't the point.

In the emerging church, the focus is on worshiping in a way that fits your culture. Maybe your community isn't ready to do Play-Doh sculpture or bang on hand drums. That's okay. The idea is to release people to do whatever it is they need to do to have a genuine encounter with God—and to facilitate those experiences.

Topic: Excavating Classical Christianity

[Posted by: ezekiel]

Hey guys,
I'm doing a conference in July talking about recovery, discovery, and the excavation of classical Christianity in the emerging church.

I'd love to hear your experiences as I prepare...

[Posted by: ultraman]

I once went to a Catholic church with my roommate on Good Friday and they did this service called the Veneration of the Cross, which was really cool. So a while later I was leading a service at my own church...and I appropriated (stole) large chunks of the Veneration liturgy (found online) as well as my own musings to make a really cool guided meditation. I had a large wooden cross in the middle of our room for us to look at while we meditated.

More and more evangelicals are experimenting with liturgy and symbolism. It's a weird world. Time-Life has spent millions to market Songs 4 Worship on TV and evangelicals are doing Veneration of the Cross. Wild!

[Posted by: talitha]

I was raised in the Methodist church, but my parents were involved in the '70s charismatic movement. I have attended churches of different denominations, but I have never been Catholic.

One of the most meaningful devotional practices I have encountered is the Catholic practice of contemplation (see Henri Nouwen's book,

With Open Hands). I understand the Quakers practice something similar in their meetings....Long silences punctuated by the input of the Lord....I also practice lectio divina in which the reader reads slowly, waiting for the "divine light" to be cast upon a word or phrase or selection. In Protestant terms, that would be letting the Holy Spirit instruct as you read. Both of these practices have deepened my walk...

[Posted by: rj24601]

One of the coolest adaptations of ancient-future things was "Catacomb Communion" with my youth group. The youth pastor read selections from Corinthians and from historical accounts of early Christians when they would sneak into the Catacombs under Rome and take communion. I don't know how historically accurate it was, but wow, it was powerful!

He covered all the windows and doors with black paper. The room was totally dark except for candles. Then we would come forward and tear off a piece of bread, dip it in this cool, old looking goblet of grape juice and find a place for prayer and meditation. We would take the bread on our own, not led by any order. The point was for us to contemplate our life of sacrifice for Christ while taking in His great sacrifice.

You know, I really didn't intend to call this book *Making Sense of Church*. My original title was *Beyond Coffee and Candles*—suggesting there's more to the postmodern story than meets the eye.

What makes a service postmodern?

What makes a church emerging? Is it the style of music? The ambiance? The flow of activities?

No.

I think it's important to recognize that introducing icons and liturgy—or even coffee and candles—won't make your church postmodern. Lots of established churches offer smells and bells, but it doesn't put them in the emerging category. Likewise, a traditional church doesn't become postmodern by suddenly bringing in electric guitars and selling its pipe organ.

While people in the emerging church are willing to try new things in worship, they are, more importantly, willing to relinquish control. The shift from teacher to facilitator means letting go and allowing the Holy Spirit to lead. It means taking the weight of the service off the pastor and, instead, celebrating everyone's gifts.

What is the job of the facilitator? It's this: To create an environment where individuals can meet with God in significant, life-changing ways. That may involve traditional preaching, or it may not.

For years, we have elevated teaching to the exclusion of other gifts. Paul described the church in terms of a body. Whether we realize it or not, we're walking around with a body that's grossly out of proportion to our head. Our obsession with teaching has made us a caricature of what God intended.

The shift from teacher to facilitator ultimately requires wrestling with our own motivations. The bitter, resentful, angry pastor is not a pretty picture—and yet it's a reality in many churches. The more worship is decentralized, the more humility is required.

After years of being the star of the show, many pastors find it hard to take a back seat and let others take the spotlight. Becoming a facilitator requires dying to pride and recognizing just how much identity we've drawn from our position of power.

At the same time, however, the facilitator model has the potential to be incredibly freeing. It effectively ends perfectionism and "pulpit envy" by removing the need for pastors to be smarter than everyone else. Rather than feeling threatened by others' talents and abilities, leaders can embrace these gifts and truly celebrate them.

As facilitators, pastors can admit where their inadequacies lie and look to others to fill in the gaps. They can rest, knowing that worship doesn't begin and end with them. Indeed, they can experience a sense of serenity and peace in their ministries.

Application

1. Where is your church on the teacher to facilitator continuum?

Teacher	Facilitator
• I believe our gatherings are primarily about passing down knowledge	• I believe we can learn from each other
• My focus is preaching	• My focus is participation
• I believe Bible teaching alone changes lives	• I believe the Lord can and prefers to use a combination of influences to change our hearts and lives
• I believe I would be failing God and my church if I didn't faithfully preach a sermon each Sunday	• I believe preaching is one way of communicating the truths of Scripture
• "I'm God's appointed leader..."	• "I'm only one of God's leaders of this community..."

2. Think for a moment of all the areas of your life where you effectively act as a "teacher." What would it look like if you were to become more of a facilitator? How would your mode of relating change?

3. Think back to ways you have embraced change. What were the circumstances? Was your learning taught, facilitated, or both?

Hero t

o Human

A Conversation about "Spiritual Growth"

Chapter 4

One of my favorite movies is *The Wizard of Oz*. Dorothy, Toto, the Tin Man, the Scarecrow, the Lion—I love them all. My favorite character, however, is the Wizard. He has all the answers, holds all the keys, and knows the way home. What more could you want?

Of course, if you've seen the movie, you know that the Wizard isn't quite what he appears to be. As Dorothy begs the Wizard to keep his promise to help her get back to Kansas, Toto sinks his teeth into a shiny green curtain and tugs. Behind the curtain Dorothy sees a small, white-haired man frantically pulling levers, turning dials, and flipping switches. It turns out the Wizard isn't a wizard at all, but an ordinary man—apparently some guy whose hot air balloon floated away at a state fair. Upon landing in Oz, however, the man quickly acclaimed himself the great and powerful Wizard of Oz. A machine helped complete the transformation by allowing him to project an alternate vision of himself—one that people respected and admired.

I don't know about you, but I identify with the Wizard. Truth be known, I too have spent much of my life hiding behind a curtain, desperately hoping some smoke and mirrors would convince people that I was bigger than I really am. Why? Because I was a pastor—and I honestly thought pastors were supposed to be successful in every area of life.

Given my theological training and educational background, you'd think that I—of all people—would understand sin and my ongoing need for a Savior. Yet, somehow, that's not the way it worked. After a few years in ministry, I lost sight of my own weaknesses. I learned to cover up my frailty and project a more polished persona to the public. Eventually, I not only fooled the people around me—I also fooled myself. When Toto pulled at the curtain on me a few years back, I was shocked at what I saw.

At the time, I had been meeting regularly with three other men. Although I had subconsciously wished my small group would help me confront my own brokenness, when it came down to it, I wasn't a very willing participant. Try as I might, I found myself reluctant to go very deep. Every now and again, I'd come up with some small sin or other to confess, but for the most part, I stayed on the fringe. I wanted to be the hero, not the struggler. Consequently, if the group learned anything about me, it was that I saw myself as an example of what a Christian leader and pastor should be.

In many ways, my less-than-honest behavior shouldn't be all that surprising. After all, modern leadership models stress cultivating a strong exterior, one that inspires confidence and devotion. Modernists, by definition, have a strong faith in the future. They're passionate about human potential and believe in the inevitability of progress. Consequently, admitting that you're weak, or have troubles as a leader, is frowned upon. It's the "Come on, be a man!" approach to life.

When it comes to spirituality, modern people believe that anything is possible if they just work hard enough. Duty and discipline are the keys to discipleship. It's important to get better, move ahead, and ultimately arrive. Got problems in your life? Get the sin out. Work hard for God and you'll get the desires of your heart. Obedience, after all, leads to blessing. God values people who are passionate about their faith and take Christianity seriously. He especially values people who aren't afraid to leap tall buildings in a single bound and are willing to run themselves ragged for the kingdom.

In many churches, the call to heroism is implied more than stated. Does God have grace for people? Absolutely, but "holiness" is equally as important. If I'm a part of this kind of spiritual community, my biggest fear will be disappointing God. I'm certain that one day I'm going to burst out of the phone booth only to find my cape is tucked into my underwear. And darn it, I should do better than that!

A few years ago, I didn't recognize any of these things. All I knew was that I wasn't prepared to spill my guts to other people, Christian or not. Still, the difficulties in my personal life persisted. Although I justified my silence for a while, eventually I just couldn't do it anymore. While my sins may have seemed small compared to others, they were sins just the same—and I knew they were destroying me. They were spiritual kryptonite to my Superman persona.

Finally overwhelmed, I invited the group to my house one evening and unveiled the reality of my life. I pulled back the curtain—certain that loathing and contempt would be my fate. Shame, humiliation, and rejection...I was ready for it all. What I found, however, was grace—and the unconditional love of Jesus Christ.

My friends came, they listened, and we prayed. They met my sin with open minds and open hearts. Instead of the anger and disapproval I expected, I received support. They told me my career was not ruined. In fact, they committed to walk with me, care for me, and help me.

Week after week, my friends held me up in the midst of my brokenness. They faithfully celebrated each step in my journey, no matter how small or insignificant. These men knew the focus had to be on the process—the journey—not the destination or final goal. After all, we are humans, not heroes.

The mental shift from hero to human has been a significant one for me—and it's even more significant in the church today. Postmodern people don't have a lot of patience for fakes. Authenticity, even if it's not pretty, is always preferred.

The following messages pick up on this theme—the quest for personal excellence and a religion that often seems out of touch with real life's messiness. How do we handle pain—our own and the pain of others?

Topic: Changes in Worship

[Posted by: moshie]

I think the defining hallmarks of postmodern worship will include a balanced view of God. Not just cheerleader songs and hailing Jesus as the answer, but also expressions of frustration, struggle, and confession. An appreciation of him "ruining" our lives and "blessing" our lives.

A friend of mine has a disability and lives in chronic pain. At his church the person leading the worship starts the service by saying: "Isn't it wonderful to be here. It feels good to praise the Lord." My friend said that he wanted to shout out: "I feel like s**t." I think his thoughts might have been a truer expression of worship than the rest of the people following a cheerleader with blank minds and hearts.

Worship should be honest—and that will make it messy. I might sing the song "I'm hungry, I'm hungry for more of you" and think, "That's crap! I'm hungrier for a steak and beer with my buddies," which could lead to repentance and confession. A quick glance at the Psalms might help in bringing balance, and honesty. Consider a worship expression based on Psalm 44 [THE MESSAGE]:

Get up, GOD! Are you going to sleep all day?
Wake up! Don't you care what happens to us?
Why do you bury your face in the pillow?
Why pretend things are just fine with us?
And here we are—flat on our faces in the dirt,
held down with a boot on our necks.
Get up and come to our rescue.

If you love us so much, Help us!

Walter Breuggemann writes in his book, The Message of the Psalms:

"It is no wonder that the church has intuitively avoided these psalms. They lead us into dangerous acknowledgement of how life really is. They lead us into the presence of God where everything is not polite and civil. They cause us to think unthinkable thoughts and utter unutterable words. Perhaps worst, they lead us away from the comfortable religious claims of 'modernity' in which everything is managed and controlled."

Praise, silence, confession, honesty, balance.
This will rock the community!

This post raises an important question: What might embracing our humanity mean for our worship events? Do we, for instance, have any honest "Where are you God?" songs in our repertoire? Songs of praise are good, but do we also know songs of lament? What about the Scriptures we choose? Do they serve to reinforce our denial or help us come clean before God?

Topic: Being Clay

[Posted by: JAK]

Generally speaking, most of the believers I know have had their spiritual lives developed most through pain and trial.

How has pain and trial affected you? What did you learn and did you notice various stages that you went through in your journey? What are the priceless nuggets of truth you have discovered as a result of going through the furnace?

Also, how many of you feel like you are in the furnace right now and need to know if anyone else can relate?

[Posted by: sharont7]

Okay—I will be honest and say suffering sucks. Plain and simple. There is no way getting around that. Yah, as Christians, God is our strength, and yah, Jesus is our only healer, but pain and sometimes the way we as Christians candy coat it makes me sick. This past year I have been put in places to experience real pain for the first time. After moving away to a new city because of God's calling, my pastor resigned, our church fell apart, I had to have surgery, a good friend was killed in a hit and run accident, and now my dad is dying of cancer.

I work at a Christian organization, and am surrounded by Christians all day long. It is a hard line to find in being real when pain hits our block. People want you to "share" your pains with them, but when you really tell them that you think life sucks right now, they don't so much act like they want to "share" in this part of your life. When pain comes in life, you quickly learn who wants to really do life with you.

[Posted by: MeAgain]

Unprepared for pain:

Ecclesiastes 3 says there is a time for everything under the sun, a time to weep and a time to laugh. I think that pain and suffering are a natural part of every person's experience. For the most part, however, people expect to be exempt from the really bad stuff and are surprised and unprepared when things go wrong.

I don't know if this is true of other cultures or not, but in middle America people are conditioned to look the other way when it comes to pain both in our expectations of experiencing pain in our own lives and in how we react to others who are in pain

Denial is rampant in the Christian community. In the modern world, there is tremendous pressure for things to be neat, tidy, and otherwise "nice." Despite all our rhetoric about loving and caring for people, it seems the church hasn't done a very good job of actually providing that kind of support. We often want people to clean up a little bit and then come back. The result? Even more pain for the hurting. Do we promise one thing and deliver another?

[Posted by: MeAgain]

Sometimes people just avoid you because they are uncomfortable. Some ask intimate questions even if you don't know them well. It is so important to find someone to share your pain with, but you don't have to share it with everyone you know: some people aren't appropriate to share pain with. Some can't handle it, some aren't intimate enough with you, some are reckless with your feelings, some don't really care when they ask how you're doing, some just ask because they want the gossip. It pays to be selective.

[Posted by: tammy]

People in pain need someone to listen to them without any of the following:

```
 •  advice  giving
 •  correction
 •  judgment
 •  telling  them  about  someone  else  who  is  worse  off
 •  making  a  joke  to  get  their  mind  off  of  it
 •  telling  them  the  solution  to  the  problem

In  other  words,  the  listener  should  LISTEN  and  NOT  TALK  SO  MUCH.
The  best  thing  you  can  do  is  listen,  say  very  little,  and  pay  for
the  coffee.
```

Heroes want to fix. Having stuffed our own pain (at least temporarily), we're quick to show you how to do the same. While no doubt this kind of behavior has always been hurtful, it's particularly offensive in the postmodern world.

I'm reminded of what Henri Nouwen wrote in *Out of Solitude*: "The friend who can be silent with us in a moment of despair or confusion, who can stay with us in an hour of grief and bereavement, who can tolerate not-knowing, not-curing, not-healing and face with us the reality of our powerlessness, that is the friend who cares."

```
[Posted  by:  JAK]

How  can  we  worship  in  Spirit  and  Truth,  when  we  don't  feel  we  can
be  honest  or  truthful  about  our  pain  and  our  current  response  to
our  life's  situation?

And  how  can  we  say  we  are  a  community  of  followers  of  Jesus
Christ  and  be  so  ignorant  about  how  to  minister  to  a  sister  in  pain?

I  also  understand  what  you  mean  by  discovering  who  really  wants  to
do  life  with  you.  Maybe  non-Christians  do  community  better  at  the
bar  or  Starbucks  because  they  don't  feel  they  will  be  judged  as  "less
than"  if  they  admit  to  life  not  being  so  great.  How  ironic  it  is  that
the  Scriptures  tell  us  that  any  "spirituality"  we  have  is  because  of
God,  but  somehow  if  we  admit  to  struggling  with  really  crappy  life
situations,  it  somehow  implies  we  are  backslidden  reprobates.


[Posted  by:  sharont7]

I  know  the  people  who  have  had  the  biggest  impact  on  my  life  have
been  people  who  were  real,  but  somehow  seemed  to  balance  the
whole  truth  part  well.

I  have  a  question  for  you  guys—when  serving  in  a  leadership  posi-
tion,  how  do  you  be  real  with  current  life  struggles,  yet  still  be  a
leader  and  encourager?  How  do  you  stay  committed  to  ministry  with
your  whole  heart  and  yet  still  deal  with  your  own  stuff?  I  feel  a
little  foolish  to  ask  these  things,  but  I  feel  so  divided  between
what  God  has  called  me  to,  and  dealing  with  my  dad  being  on  his
death  bed  in  another  state.
```

Topic: Reversing the Stereotype

[Posted by: DesertPastor]

It seems that Christians are frequently stereotyped as:
* hypocritical
* condescending
* judgmental
* intolerant
* religious wackos

Although stereotypes are usually one-dimensional overstatements, I think there's usually some amount of truth to them.

So what would happen IF the negative stereotype associated with "Christians" began to change? What IF Christians began to be viewed in stereotypically positive ways instead of negative ones?

What practical, pragmatic, "rubber-meets-the-road" ideas do you have for reversing the negative stereotype frequently associated with Christians?

[Posted by: walking]

Wouldn't it help if we quit pointing to the big-name preachers, or even our local pastor, as the success stories and start pointing to Jesus? I KNOW Jesus isn't going to let them down!

The modern "testimony" often seems contrived to postmodern people. It seems more like a sales pitch for Jesus than an honest account of God's work in a person's life. Heroes are inherently hard to relate to because they give the impression that their lives are perfect. The people around them inevitably feel less than, as though there's something wrong with them. Humans, meanwhile, are loveable even with their weaknesses. And yet, how often do we hear testimonies from humans—those who are still in process?

[Posted by: godseeker]

How many times have I (we) been so busy in ministry and Christian stuff that I've run over people in my way? And how many times have I (we) been so focused on communicating specific info or getting a person to a different viewpoint that we've totally objectified him or her?

I'm making time for people. I'm trying to be there for them when they need it and letting them be there for me as well, rather than gritting my teeth and trying to be a "spiritual superman who would never stoop to being helped by heathen." (ugh)

I'm also trying to show people how close they are to God rather than how far they are from him.

[Posted by: iphigeneia]

I think it's easier to look at other people's flaws/shortcomings than our own. I think honesty scares us. It threatens to destroy us—and yet we miss so much by not allowing ourselves to be destroyed.

Formulas are tangible. Quick phrases and schedules and trademarked terms are tangible. They have a weight to them simply because they are. We hardly have to work with them—we can just point to them as proof.

The cry for authenticity is hard to miss in these posts. Increasingly, people are desperate to come out of hiding. Yet in many cases, their church isn't a safe place to do that. Again, how might transitioning from the hero to human model impact the way we interact with people? This next post uses poetry to create an even more compelling picture.

Topic: Poetry Anyone?

[Posted by: beks]

Cry of the Broken

The scene lay open before me
as I walked through the path of rubble,
walls of a fortress once impenetrable by all.
It appeared to be a war-torn city, left for dead, left in ruin and ash.
Climbing over the brokenness, an amazing beauty arose;
beauty from the ashes,
joy from brokenness.

The walls built to protect, became my prison, I built my death.
My heart screamed for freedom at the Jericho in which my mind dwelled.
Somewhere was a Promised Land waiting—joy to rise from the rubble.

I walked around and around these walls...remembering the scars that built them and the false security they contained.

Brick by brick, stone by stone I turned to face fear itself...
I drew a deep breath in, compelled by one desire,
to be captured by grace and set free by joy.
More than breath I reached for brokenness.

```
One by one the stones began to crumble to the ground
fire consumed this ash
exposed, innocent, broken
fire consumed this heart
taking each piece and creating joy
building a temple meek and humble
dependent yet strengthened through the fire

A fortress destroyed by a cry of the broken
brought true joy to the heart of a servant.
The trials of the world encamped around
are no longer knocking at the door.
Fear is no longer holding the key.
For the Lord has captured my heart
torn down my Jericho and replaced it with joy.
```

Holding the hero image in our heads often sends us down the same path as the Pharisees. The Pharisees, after all, were all about looking good. They went to great lengths to appear righteous before each other and the wider spiritual community. And yet what did Jesus say to them? "You are like whitewashed tombs, which look beautiful on the outside but on the inside are full of dead men's bones and everything unclean" (Matthew 23:27). Indeed, Jesus reserved his harshest words for the people who insisted on hiding their brokenness.

In Luke 18:9–14, Jesus tells the story of two men praying. One, a Pharisee, stands up and prays, "God, I thank you that I am not like other men—robbers, evildoers, adulterers—or even like this tax collector. I fast twice a week and give a tenth of all I get." The tax collector meanwhile, stands at a distance. He beats his breast and says simply, "God, have mercy on me, a sinner." Jesus makes his point very clear: "I tell you that this man, rather than the other, went home justified before God. For everyone who exalts himself will be humbled, and he who humbles himself will be exalted."

The reality is Jesus came into the world to address the issue of brokenness. What's more, his grace is sufficient for us throughout our lives, not merely at the moment of "salvation." But somehow, we've lost sight of this idea. In our modern quest for success, we've begun faking our sanctification. Believing we should have "arrived" as Christians long ago, we become chameleons and charlatans. Like the Wizard, we present a false self to the world—one that we think people will honor, respect, and, most importantly, love. This persona has sin licked and struggles less and less. It appears, for all intents and purposes, to be "spiritually mature."

The problem with the hero image, however, is that it doesn't drive us to Jesus Christ. Instead, it causes us to draw on our own resources. Ironically, we choose to present a false self to the world believing it will keep us safe—yet, sadly, it imprisons. It inhibits spiritual growth by cutting us off from experiencing God's provision of grace. It keeps us isolated in our sin, desperately trying to keep the mask from slipping.

In my own life, I've had to re-evaluate what "a good Christian" looks like. I've come to believe that wholeness comes not through trying harder, but by admitting my weaknesses and trusting God for the healing journey. The only way I can grow in my spiritual life is by taking off the mask and going skin to skin with God.

My daughter Grace was born at 27 weeks and weighed just 1 pound, 13 ounces. She came into the world by emergency C-section after my wife Lisa had already spent a month in the hospital on straight bed rest. It was an excruciating time for us. Three hours after Grace was born, they put Lisa in a wheelchair and rushed us to the neonatal unit to allow us to say goodbye to our tiny infant daughter. There she was in an incubator, just thirteen inches long, laden with tubes and monitors.

Miraculously, Grace pulled through that day. And the next. And the day after that. When she was one month old, I finally got to hold her. They called it "kangarooing." I can still remember opening up my shirt and resting Grace on my chest, monitors and tubes cascading from her frail body. It was an amazing experience. After only a few moments, her vital signs perked up. Her heart rate and breathing became stronger. It was as though she literally became healthier by being connected to us. This kangarooing time seemed to be an integral part of her healing.

In a sense, that's how it is with us. Being connected to God—going skin to skin with our creator in our most vulnerable and difficult moments—is what helps us move toward wholeness. And yet often, we're so disgusted by our sin that we do exactly the opposite. Rather than run toward God, we run away. It's crazy. First John 1:8 makes it so clear: "If we claim to be without sin, we deceive ourselves and the truth is not in us." Then he says it again in verse 10, in case we missed it the first time: "If we claim we have not sinned, we make him out to be a liar and his word has no place in our lives."

Sin is not only a fact of life, it's a guarantee. It's the one thing we all have in common with each other. We've sinned, we sin, and we'll sin again. So why do we pretend otherwise?

Why are we so reluctant to admit our own need? Could it be that we have yet to really grasp God's immense love for us? That we think we have something to lose by admitting who we really are?

Indeed, moving from hero to human requires not just honesty, but faith—a faith in God's provision for our weaknesses. And not just once, but throughout our lives. The tragedy of the prodigal son story is not that he sinned, but that it took him so long to admit it and run back home.

Application

1. Where are you on the continuum between hero and human?

Hero   Human

- I believe I should be a model for others
- My focus is achieving
- I believe God is disappointed in me when I sin
- I believe obedience leads to blessing and that God values hard work
- "I'm not really that bad..."

- I believe it's okay to be broken
- My focus is process
- I believe sin is an opportunity for God to draw me into deeper relationship
- I believe that Jesus' death paid my debt and I don't need to add to it through hard work
- "I'm more sinful than I realize, but also more loved"

2. In what ways have you been less than honest about your sin?

3. How would transitioning from hero to human affect your relationships? Your church?

Chapter 5

Consumer to Steward

A Conversation about "Ministry"

Oprah calls them light bulb moments. They're the times when you realize something about yourself—for better or worse—and your life changes as a result. So here's what I've learned. Ready?

I'm selfish.

Truth be known, you probably are too.

Blame it on having a sinful nature or living in a self-centered culture. For whatever reason, caring for ourselves comes easier than caring for others. Rarely are we thinking, How can I be a good steward?

I've come face to face with my selfishness a few times, but some occasions have more memorable moments than others. For instance, in 1982 I had the opportunity to work as a photographer in the Ivory Coast. Although I didn't speak any French, I didn't think twice about going. After all, wasn't English the international language? Lots of English speakers would be around, right?

Wrong. When I got there, I discovered the only people who spoke English were the missionaries with whom I was staying and the guide who had been assigned to me. Even in Abidjan, the capital, it was solid French. French newspapers, French movies, French radio and television. I couldn't even get the BBC.

Everywhere I traveled it was the same: hot, dirty, dusty, and crowded. The language barrier, combined with heat and humidity, made even simple tasks difficult. My trips to the rural areas were the worst. You'd think seeing such incredible poverty would have made me more grateful for how much I did have, but any gratitude I felt was usually short-lived. Sure I was fortunate to have a TV and toilet at the mission house, but couldn't God do something about the food?

I've always been a bit of a finicky eater, I guess, but after only a few days in Africa, I began to dream of McDonald's hamburgers, crispy fries, and ice-cold sodas. I even dreamed of broccoli and meat loaf. On my birthday, I finally gave in. I splurged and went to the local hotel. I can still remember walking into the dining room thinking how nice it would be to finally have a real dinner.

When my meal came, it wasn't too bad. The dessert, however—the one thing I'd wanted more than anything else—was a complete bust. Apparently it's a local custom to top ice cream with a sour concoction to counteract the sweetness. To this day, I'm still not sure what I ate. All I know is it tasted awful. I put my spoon down and almost burst into tears. My waiter, the hotel, the job, the country—none of it was living up to my expectations. I just wanted to go home.

In general, I found life in Africa exasperating and confusing. One day in the marketplace I took a photo of a tall man who seemed to be well-respected by those around him. I didn't ask permission to take his photo or even inquire who he was, I simply pressed the shutter. It was a great shot. How could I resist? The commotion was immediate. People began yelling and screaming and grabbing at my camera. Though I couldn't understand the words, it was obvious I'd done something wrong. Even my guide was alarmed. He grabbed me, put us in a taxi, and told the driver to speed up. Turns out, I'd taken a picture of a local Muslim leader—and in so doing, completely disregarded Muslim laws concerning human representation. Even once I understood my mistake, I remained shaken.

When the summer finally drew to a close, I was more than ready to go back to the comforts of life in America. Before I left, however, I decided to attend a Sunday service with my missionary hosts. Like many churches in Africa, the church had a thatched roof, dirt floor, and sporadic electricity. Surrounding the church was the usual assortment of chicken coops, scraggly plants, and free-running children. Once again, I was the only one who didn't speak French.

By the third hour of the service, I no longer felt spiritual. I was hot, bored, and miserable. Didn't these people know how uncomfortable I was? Why had I agreed to come to this service in the first place? The bench was killing my back and my legs were aching. Then suddenly in the midst of all my whining, I noticed everyone staring at me. They laughed and pointed. The minister looked directly at me and kept talking. What was he saying? I wondered.

In the car afterward, I learned I wasn't being laughed at so much as honored. Apparently, the pastor had explained to the people how I could have been at home, eating steak and drinking wine. Instead, I chose to come to the Ivory Coast—to be among God's people, sharing my talents with them. He went on to explain how the communion loaf was symbolic of the unity we have in Jesus Christ. A variety of grains are ground, kneaded, and baked together to create a unique taste and flavor. Once the loaf has been through the fire, we can no longer identify a Spencer, a missionary, or a farmer. Instead, we are one loaf—and we serve one purpose: to feed and nourish those around us. We share each other's joys and hardships. When one part suffers, we all suffer.

Something in the pastor's words touched me at a deep level. He not only gave me a new way to think about what it means to be a Christian, he also helped me recognize my self-interest for what it was. It was truly a "light bulb moment."

Am I proud of how I behaved in Africa? Not at all. In fact, it's embarrassing to retell the story. It reveals how arrogant, gluttonous, and ungrateful I am. I was surrounded by abject poverty. Yet all I could do was whine about how heavy my gear was—and how harsh it was to not have ice cubes in my drinks. How could my perspective have been so skewed?

Over the years, I've come to see how much I take for granted and how terribly demanding I am. I'm the quintessential consumer. So often, my primary concern is myself—my needs, my interests, my family, my health and safety. The rest of the world can go to hell, literally, so long as my comfort is maintained. I call myself a follower of Jesus Christ, but am I really? Do I really know what it means to love?

I think we could ask the same questions of our churches. Think about it. How many of our ministries are about serving ourselves? How much of our budget is spent on programs, events, classes, and seminars to feed our flock?

Not sure?

Let me ask the question another way. How many of our ministries are about serving people outside the congregation? What percentage of the overall budget is directed toward the community—other groups or other nations? My guess is not too much.

As I travel and talk with people, there seems to a growing sense of frustration with our churches. Christians are beginning to question our lack of stewardship and involvement in compassionate ministry.

Indeed, these days the word "ministry" has become synonymous with "program." Truth be known, we seldom think of doing "ministry" apart from church. I mean, with Sunday school classes, morning and evening services, prayer meetings, Bible studies, small group meetings, and committees, who has time for anything else?

Yet the metaphor of the steward would suggest that it's my responsibility to give back at least as much as I take. Sure, God gave us the earth to subdue and rule over, but ruling doesn't mean hoarding and exploiting. Material blessings are just that—blessings, to be shared with the whole community. Not only does the church need to be a good steward of its resources, I need to be a good steward, as well—spending my money wisely and making the most of my time and God-given gifts.

It's fascinating to me to see how relative the sin of gluttony has become. Who are the gluttons? Well, the people who have more than me, of course. It rarely occurs to me to think that I might be in that category—that perhaps I might be taking more from this world than I legitimately need. Of course, challenge me on my greed and I'm apt to tell you how much I tithe—how faithfully I give to the church's "ministries." Whose job is it to care for the poor? The church's, of course. Feeding the poor isn't something we do as part of our daily lives. It's a weekend event—a special project we might take on once a month in the same way we plan bowling and movie nights.

In Matthew 16:24, Jesus told the disciples: "If anyone would come after me, he must deny himself and take up his cross and follow me." The question, of course, is what does that really mean? What would it mean if we were to give up our consumer mentality and instead interact with the world as a steward?

Topic: Christian Culture is Dead

[Posted by: footer]

Christian culture is dead. Like the great Cathedrals of Europe, it's a nice place to visit, but nothing alive is happening there—it's a picture of the past. Our Christian music, candy bars, books—the whole thing is one big festering carcass plugged into the consumer life support system and no one is willing to pull the plug. Each year Christians (especially in America) chunk billions into the Christian Culture machine, buying the Christian brand, and what do we have to show for it? Have we made an impact for Jesus Christ?

Every week millions sit in things called worship services next to those they do not know, hearing from those that do not know them. The tithe has become a modern indulgence, paying for someone else to do the works of Christ in the world. Worship itself has become nothing more than a smorgasbord, a spiritual buffet, based more upon the current musical style and emotion than the real awe of God. In our American Bandstand mentality, we rank our worship as if it were something that could or should be measured.

Discipleship has little or nothing to do with life...The words of Jesus have no meaning for us in reality. He has saved us for heaven only, and His words need to be spiritualized or made into self-improvement mantra to be grasped. He surely didn't mean those things he said! He surely didn't mean for us to give up our possessions—not really. He didn't mean for us to invite homeless people into our homes—surely not! He could not have told us to give more to those who steal from us—how could he? How could anyone accept that?

We talk about evangelism. How to do it. Why to do it. What words to say. What words not to say. We practice it with diagrams and charts. We have the steps all laid out. But do our lives overflow with the grace and love of Jesus Christ?

[Posted by: madison]

The lie sold by the secular and Christian culture is that you need to buy things. You need the newest self help book or the latest installment in the Left Behind series blah blah blah. How do we decon-struct this myth, this lie of Christian consumerism? How do we relate to the world somewhere between an ascetic monk and worshiping the golden calf of consumerism? Personally, I say stop shopping at Wal-Mart. Find out how what you're buying affects the rest of the world our brothers and sisters in China and elsewhere.

These first few posts hit straight to the point. What does it mean to be a follower of Jesus Christ in a consumer culture? How has consumerism changed the ministry of the church? Does being a steward just mean saying goodbye to "Jesus Junk"? Or is there more to it?

[Posted by: footer]

Maybe when I'm talking about Christian culture I'm partly talking about the marketing, about the empty hype of it all...Christianity, Inc., or The Church. But it goes deeper than just products.

I wonder sometimes if what we're talking about is pseudo-Christianity, pseudo-Discipleship. Think about this. Person A goes on a mission trip. He goes because of the church's push on involve-ment, and he thinks it will be a good experience for him. He goes and spends a week serving the poor and suddenly feels like someone who cares for the poor. He comes back and tells everyone what a great experience it was. He tells everyone they need to go next year. He goes back to work. He goes back to his family. He goes back to his normal job. And the missions experience becomes a memory and a yearly trip.

Here's another scenario. Worship. Person B goes to a worship service. She sings. She cries. She prays. She's moved inside. She can feel God. She leaves. She goes home. She goes back to her normal life. Worship for her is a memory and a weekly program.

Are Person A and Person B disciples? Does Person A really care about the poor, or does he just feel like he cares about the poor? Is Person B really a worshipper, or just someone who feels like a worshipper?

It's like buying a four-wheel-drive off-road vehicle because I want to feel like an outdoorsy guy (which the commercial clearly makes it seem like I will be if I own one). But am I outdoorsy? Or just the same lame guy driving an expensive car?

We have to get past the facades of all our empty programs and hype. Past the Christianity of events and into the life.

What does most of what we do have to do with the Kingdom?

I love Footer's point here about pseudo-discipleship. Missions trips aren't bad necessarily, nor is Sunday worship. The question, though, is: Are we helping people to eventually grow beyond the program? Or are we "enabling" them to stay where they are and, in some way, feeding their addiction? This next thread picks up on this idea. Why do people come to church anyway? And why do they leave?

Topic: Reasons people leave church

[Posted by: preachinjesus]

We have seen a host of reasons why people leave church here in downtown Fort Worth. One family told us they weren't coming to our church any more because they "wanted their kids to have more playtime" and church infringed upon that. At least one young guy was honest enough to tell us that he was too drunk on Sunday mornings to even contemplate finding a pair of pants, much less making his way down the road to church. People's reasons for leaving church are numerous. Some are justified and some aren't.

I have also seen people leave churches based on the biggest, best, and most unbelievable Sunday service each week because they get "bored." A friend of mine said if you want church to be a circus show, you better either have an incredible ringmaster (i.e., senior pastor) or a great show that gets bigger and better.

Reasons people leave churches are numerous. What reasons do we give them to stay may be something worthwhile to looking into.

[Posted by: the_soulsurfer]

I believe our CULTURE is partly to blame. We live in a technological/media driven society. This society has produced a generation of people who are relationally retarded. We don't know HOW to do relationships...because we have been trained to be self-centric consumers. Church is practiced by self-centric consumers, and marketed to self-centric consumers....and that's the rub. We aren't practiced in community, in knowing how to care for others above ourselves. We have all been trained to think that the next thing we try will satisfy our desire, whether that's an Ab-Flex or a church. When it doesn't, we sink back into our cubicle of isolated pain, waiting for the next commercial.

[Posted by: liquidthinking]

People leave churches because....

1. the pastor had an affair
2. someone sitting near them had bad gas
3. the children's ministry sucked
4. the pastor stopped preaching good sermons
5. God told them to leave
6. they talked too much about money
7. they didn't talk enough about money
8. they weren't growing
9. the music was too loud
10. the music was not loud enough
11. the pastor drank beer
12. they had no sense of color when decorating
13. too diverse a crowd
14. crowd wasn't diverse enough
15. the crucifix was big and scary
16. pastor didn't preach Scripture
17. pastor read the Bible too much
18. I'm allergic to Hypocrites
19. they didn't help the poor enough
20. all they talked about was the poor
21. there wasn't enough parking
22. there was too much parking—I had to walk too far
23. the preacher was monotone
24. the preacher yelled too much
25. they were unorganized
26. they ran the place like a business
27. the hymnals should have been blue
28. they wouldn't let me bring my pet to church
29. church signs are stupid
30. Adam did not have a belly button

Some people leave the institution we call church and grow closer to Jesus. I am one.

Every time I see this list, I can't help but laugh—then cry. In today's culture, people literally shop for churches. If the megachurch 45 minutes away has great worship, we'll get on the freeway and drive there. If the community church across town has a good children's program, we'll go there. No one has yet told us: "Ask not what your church can do for you, but what you can do for your church."

[Posted by: JAK]

The other day I stopped in to my favorite hang out—Joe's Grill & Bar. I go to Joe's to catch a game (I don't get cable), have a beer, and study the people. Anyway, when I went in I noticed they had redecorated. I liked it. For some time I had thought the place needed some sprucing up.

There was a sign, "Under new management". Hmmm. When my waitress came, it wasn't one that I knew. I had been developing good relationships with many of them and they were comfortable sharing their lives with me when business was slow. Actually, all the staff looked new.

I took the menu and discovered the new cook changed the old menu. I couldn't order my favorite chicken strips any more—I substituted my chicken strips for something else and ordered a beer. "Sorry, we don't have that special anymore," my waitress told me. Another disappointment.

About this time the band starts warming up and for the next 45 minutes makes nothing but senseless noise as they check their sound system. It bugged the heck out of me. I couldn't wait to leave.

In my car I thought to myself, "This sucks." My place was no more. I no longer felt the same feelings....Nothing was familiar and I didn't enjoy anything but the new decor.

It then dawned on me: This is what happens in church after church across America. New managers come in or hop on a new way of doing church, change staff, change the music—take away the familiar and replace it with something different.

I'm not saying that churches shouldn't make changes, but I am saying we have to understand people's need to feel like it's their church to have a place of belonging.

I have tried Joes's three more times. Each time was no better than the first. I have decided not to complain to the new manager; I'll just take my business elsewhere and find a new favorite place to belong.

Here's the "Yeah, but" post. As JAK points out, sometimes people leave churches for legitimate reasons. While we need to acknowledge the dangers of consumerism, we can't just ignore what people want either. After all, the church exists for people—the people who are there and the people who are not (i.e., those to whom we are called to minister in this world). The challenge, of course, is to find a balance.

Topic: Christian Culture Is Dead

[Posted by: footer]

What if our churches are nothing but products to be consumed?

Scene 1, Churches R Us counter

Teller: Could I help you?

Customer: Yeah, I'd like a church.

Teller: What size? Mega, Regular, or small group?

Customer: Well...make it small group.

Teller: What flavor? Traditional, Contemporary, or PoMo?

Customer: What's the difference between Contemporary and PoMo—don't they both have good music?

Teller: On Contemporary we hold the angst and add the color coordination....

Customer: Hh, yes, then make it a PoMo...color coordination has never set well with my stomach...but heavy on the angst.

Teller: Okay then, one PoMo Small Group church (extra angst)...would you like anything else with that? We have a special on "cutting-edge" feelings with our PoMo churches today.

Customer: Okay, I'll have one of those too.

Scene 2, Churches R Us eating area

Customer 1 (after angst drips from the church onto his shirt): Ah crap, now I've got angst all over me!

Customer 2 (smiling at next table): Yep, that angst always makes a mess.

Let's face it. Ministry is messy—especially in the postmodern context. I also find it interesting how often we get ministry and style mixed up. If I hear anything in these posts, it's this: Let's move away from doing church (i.e., having conversations about color coordination and small groups) and be the church (i.e., focus on the things that really mattered to Jesus). There seems to be a desire to de-centralize—to make ministry something that everyone is responsible for, not just the pastor. The next thread picks up on this idea. What does stewardship look like in everyday life? What happens when ministry moves outside the confines of the church?

Topic: Homeless dilemma

[Posted by: jugdish]

My wife and I were on the road this evening on our way to LA. We stopped for gas in Bakersfield and came across a woman with a wheelbarrow full of plastic bottles and cans. She also had a sign that read, "Hungry, please help." I didn't notice the sign until on my way out of the gas station. When I got to the car I was left with a perplexing question, "What can I do?" I began a conversation about this with my wife on the road and we couldn't come to any resolution. So, I pose this question: In the five minutes that I was at the gas station, what could I have done that would have left an impact on this woman? Is there anything that we can do in our everyday encounters with people, homeless or not, that will leave a lasting impact on them?

[Posted by: footer]

I have varying thoughts on this topic....

First, I think the big thing is to be led by the Spirit. That's the picture I see of Jesus in these situations....doing what He sees the Father doing.

Second, I think true compassion has to go beyond the "hit-and-run-I'm-glad-I-can-help-someone" moments. If I were a homeless guy, I think I'd think someone was a prick for getting their "do-gooder" kicks by spending a few moments with me to "help me." So beyond those led by the Spirit moments where something more wonderful than the trivial could happen, I think that Jesus Christ has called his people to give their lives for those in need. The Matthew 25 passages combined with Isaiah 58 make it very clear that God wants us to not just give moments but to share our lives with the hungry, poor, naked, and homeless. Christ left all to rescue us from our poverty...he did not make a pit stop on the rat-race of self-indulgence. This is our model.

Third, quit giving to your Church. Instead, tithe....I mean tithe like the Scriptures tell us. God's desire for the gifts of his people was to help those who had no inheritance. The gifts (which were mostly foodstuffs—animals and grain) were brought to the storehouse for those in need in the community....Wouldn't it be great if the church was known more for raising money and sharing life with those in need than for using their fund-raising campaigns to build buildings?

```
[Posted by: jackiewyse]

Life is a seamless garment. When one person suffers, we all suffer.
When we ignore the suffering around us, we are cutting ourselves
off from the essential connections that are an inherent part of
how God created this beautifully complex world. Your suffering is
mine, mine is yours. Reaching out to grasp the hand of the other
is, in a very real way, also reaching toward our own healing. This is
not selfishness (it's all about me) as much as it is humility (I am
connected and affected and MOVED by all who surround me).

Of course, there is the problem of boundaries. How do we live into
this vision of compassion (for others, for ourselves) and humility
and service without getting burned out?
```

I love what Jackiewyse says here about life being a seamless garment. That's really the point that was driven home to me in Africa. When I see myself as a steward, I'm more likely to do acts of compassion. Not because I feel guilty, or because it's "the right thing to do," but because I genuinely feel the pain of other people. I see myself as part of something much bigger. And yet it's interesting how the issue of boundaries comes up. Why is it, I wonder, that we feel the need to be clear about where one person ends and another begins? Is it because we fear that we'll be consumed by the people around us?

Topic: Bono in Christianity Today

```
[Posted by: preachinjesus]

I just got through reading the latest issue of Christianity Today
where the cover article is on Bono....The article was dealing primarily
with Bono's quest to address the AIDS epidemic in Africa....

Do you think AIDS is an issue the Church should respond to? How should
the Church respond?


[Posted by: walking]

May I express a high level of pisstivity at the general church in
America today for just a moment?

When did we (the church) get into the business of deciding which
diseases and which afflictions God should heal and which peoples we
should help? As if even the best of us is better than anyone with
AIDS. People are dying and many preachers/pastors are spending
time in the pulpit arguing that AIDS isn't really the problem that
AIDS "activists" claim it is. People are dying by the millions AND
THE CHURCH, FOR THE MOST PART, DOESN"T CARE! The attitude is
it's not an acceptable disease—so let 'em die.
```

I think AIDS is one of many issues that the world will look back on and ask, "Where was the church?" Like it or not, I think we will be judged on how we handle the crisis. At present, our actions don't match up with our words. Our silence on the issue—and our lack of concern for the growing number of widows and orphans—is deafening. We talk about having love and compassion for the people of the world, but continue to pour the vast majority of our resources into ourselves—our church buildings and our programs. While we're paving parking lots and building auditoriums, African children are literally lying next to the corpses of their parents. It's tragic.

A thought for Lent from Isaiah 58:
Shout out, do not hold back!
    Lift up your voice like a trumpet!
Announce to my people their rebellion,
    to the house of Jacob their sins.
Yet day after day they seek me
    and delight to know my ways,
as if they were a nation that practiced righteousness
    and did not forsake the ordinance of their God;
they ask of me righteous judgments,
    they delight to draw near to God.
'Why do we fast, but you do not see?
    Why humble ourselves, but you do not notice?'
Look, you serve your own interest on your fast-day,
    and oppress all your workers.
Look, you fast only to quarrel and to fight
    and to strike with a wicked fist.
Such fasting as you do today
    will not make your voice heard on high.
Is such the fast that I choose,
    a day to humble oneself?
Is it to bow down the head like a bulrush,
    and to lie in sackcloth and ashes?
Will you call this a fast,
    a day acceptable to the LORD?
Is not this the fast that I choose:
    to loose the bonds of injustice,
    to undo the thongs of the yoke,
to let the oppressed go free,
    and to break every yoke?
Is it not to share your bread with the hungry,
    and bring the homeless poor into your house;
when you see the naked, to cover them,
    and not to hide yourself from your own kin?
Then your light shall break forth like the dawn,
    and your healing shall spring up quickly;
your vindicator shall go before you,
    the glory of the LORD shall be your rearguard.
Then you shall call, and the LORD will answer;
    you shall cry for help, and he will say, Here I am.
If you remove the yoke from among you,
    the pointing of the finger, the speaking of evil,
if you offer your food to the hungry
    and satisfy the needs of the afflicted,
then your light shall rise in the darkness
    and your gloom be like the noonday.

Topic: Should God's Will Be Dangerous?

[Posted by: DesertPastor]

At a recent leadership luncheon, Erwin McManus (pastor of Mosaic and author of An Unstoppable Force) boldly challenged the myth that "the safest place you can be—is when you're in the middle of God's will." To the contrary, McManus asserted that living in God's will is a dangerous proposition, often involving great risk. One might conclude that the lack of such risk-taking has been one of the factors contributing to the modern church's decline.

What do you think? Is God's will a place of safety, or one of danger?

This is yet another "rubber hits the road" post. It's fascinating how ministry has moved from a vagabond "Sell all your possessions and follow me" journey to "Oh, you know, Tuesday night is bad for me, can we move it to Wednesday?" Safety, convenience, reputation—how much are we willing to let go to follow Jesus?

[Posted by: chickenfriedfunk]

I read an article in the local newspaper a few years ago about a family that attended an Assembly of God church. The family was comprised of a husband, a wife, and a couple daughters, I think. They lived in a normal suburban neighborhood. At some point, they began opening their home to transients. One or two people would stay with them every night. They let them shower, fed them breakfast, maybe helped them out with a specific need, and let them go on their way. The news writer asked if they were worried that one of the transients might steal from them or assault or kill them, especially considering they have two young daughters. The parents said that this is what Jesus Christ commanded his people to do, and they are just obeying him. They said that, so far, the worst thing that had happened was one of the transients stole $5 off of their daughter's dresser. Are we to put ourselves and our families in that kind of danger? I'm thinking the answer is "yes," but I tremble at the thought of putting that into practice.

.... Are we to balance our works with mitigation of the danger those works put us in, or are we to ignore that danger? If a homeless guy that you didn't know from Adam knocked on your door, would you let him stay with you, your spouse, and your kids for a period of time?

[Posted by: ecscrubb]

If God called you to the middle of the jungle to serve a tribe of cannibals, would you go? And would you take your wife? The entire point of you going into the jungle could be for you to get martyred, have a little blurb written about it in a local paper, which

some grad student then stumbles across accidentally, gets saved,
and becomes the next Christian hero. Sure, this is a little far-
fetched, but the point is that I believe we're all pawns in God's great
design. Our choice is whether we let God move us into danger from
the other side's queen and rook, or we run fleeing from the board.

---QUOTED---
If a homeless guy that you didn't know from Adam knocked on your
door, would you let him stay with you, your spouse, and your kids
for a period of time?
---END QUOTE---

The sad reality is no, I probably would not. Not because I am or am
not "called" into that kind of ministry, but because I'm generally a
selfish person and don't help my fellow man nearly as much as I should.

[Posted by: tammy]

My husband's dad did this all the time in the 1960s and '70s. My
husband often woke up for school not knowing who would be sleeping
on the couch. It was often a stranger. His dad went so far as to
hand out his address to people and tell them that the door is
always open. If it's late, just walk in and sleep on the couch.
Sometimes that happened.

I lock my door. I work in mental health, and I've seen people who
will hurt you, thinking that they are doing a good thing. Their
thoughts are so mixed up that they don't realize at times that
they are doing harm.

But that's not to say that Jim's dad was wrong. Maybe he was just
braver than I am.

In Matthew 7, Jesus tells the story of two men: one built his house on the rock, the other on the sand. As I think about modern church, it strikes me that we're more like the latter. We've done a lot of things in Jesus name, but we've forgotten the most important rules of real estate: location, location, location. Foolishly, we've focused our attention on physical walls—and the "ministry" that can happen behind them. We look good, but our foundation is shaky.

When I was a kid, I had a pretty elaborate fort. I had curtains, furniture—the works. I even made a little fireplace by piling up some old bricks. A while later, I decided to cover the rough wood of the walls in fabric—you know, to make the place really comfortable. Then one day I found some kindling and struck a match. The fire didn't take long to catch. In fact, soon the whole fort was blazing. Panic-stricken, I ran to get water. To my horror, I realized the garden house didn't reach that far. Ever heard the saying about storming the gates of hell with a squirt gun? That's pretty much how I felt.

The problem was, my fireplace wasn't real. There was no chimney; it was just a pile of bricks. It looked good on the outside, but it was useless. That afternoon I watched as everything I had worked so hard to build burned to the ground.

I wonder if we've made a similar error in the North American church. For years, we've been preoccupied with buildings and décor, musical styles, "ministry" programs, and events. But by doing so, we've successfully isolated ourselves from the reality of the world around us. AIDS, genocide, hunger...they're news stories, far removed from our everyday reality.

This past fall, I had the opportunity to sit down with Heather Reynolds, the nurse who founded God's Golden Acre, a home for AIDS orphans in Durban, South Africa. We invited her to speak at Soularize (our annual TheOoze convention) and were thrilled when she accepted.

Heather's "ministry" began in 1993. She was visiting Uganda when she came across a deserted village. Something was troubling about the scene. A baby's cry was heard from one of the huts. Heather asked her Ugandan travel companion what was going on. She was told the child was one of a dozen or so children left behind by parents who died of AIDS. These children were starving, exhausted, and worst of all, forgotten. Heather was distraught and called her husband Patrick. "What shall I do?" she cried. "What sort of cruel world do we live in?"

Back in South Africa, Heather researched the crisis and quickly discovered that the number of AIDS orphans was escalating rapidly in her own country. Today, God's Golden Acre is home to 72 AIDS orphans, ages birth to 16 years. This past Christmas, Oprah Winfrey visited the orphanage and organized an amazing Christmas celebration there.

"Before my trip, I was shut down about the AIDS story in Africa," Oprah wrote in O Magazine (April 2003). "Like you, I'd heard the numbers—millions of children homeless, one in three people ravaged by the disease in some countries—but I was numb to what those figures represented. The statistics had just stopped registering for me...." The trip, wrote Oprah, "was the greatest single experience of my lifetime."

When I see the photographs from that trip, I can't help but get emotional. For one thing, Heather Reynolds arrived at Soularize hoping to meet Oprah. It was her first visit to the United States and she was determined to make the most of her time here. Apparently, that determination paid off. Quite apart from that, I look at those photographs and one word comes to my mind: ministry.

If Jesus were walking the earth today, I wonder what he'd do with the disciples.

Would he gather them up in a church basement somewhere for yet another Bible study? Or would he be at God's Golden Acre, bringing joy with Oprah? Does knowledge change people? Or does experience?

To be honest, before meeting Heather, I'd pretty much assumed we'd dealt with the AIDS crisis. After all, AIDS didn't seem to be affecting my life in any way, so I assumed everything was okay. I was thinking like a consumer—sitting in my little fort, seemingly safe and secure. It was only when I met Heather, and heard the heart-breaking stories firsthand, that I understood how wrong I'd been. I suddenly saw myself as part of the seamless garment mentioned earlier. The pain of Africa was my pain, too, whether I realized it or not. I had come full circle—back to that communion service in the Ivory Coast. We are one body.

Does becoming a steward mean only doing compassionate, social-action type ministry or working to protect the environment? I don't think so. Again, I think we need to be wary of swinging the pendulum too far in either direction. At the same time, however, we need to take a hard look at what we call "ministry." As Footer said earlier, how much of what we do relates to the kingdom? We ask God to bless our work, but have we ignored doing the work he's already blessed—caring for the widows and orphans, the poor and broken?

In the church today, we have an opportunity to make different choices than our parents and grandparents. "'Everything is permissible'—but not everything is beneficial," wrote Paul in 1 Corinthians 10:23. The question is what things are we willing to give up? What will stewardship look like not just in the church, but in our own lives as well? Are we willing to come out of our forts and let our hearts be touched by the pain around us? Or will we continue to use our resources on ourselves until the fire is at our doorstep?

I think about Jesus' interaction with the rich young ruler. On the surface, the young man had a lot going for him. He had money, prestige, and power. To the naked eye, he was upright and ambitious, the kind of guy you'd want endorsing your religion. And yet Jesus looked deeply into that man's heart and saw that his soul had been captured by something other than the kingdom. When Jesus gave the man an opportunity to leave his consumer lifestyle and discover real life in Jesus Christ, however, the man turned him down. In the end, the rich young ruler had almost everything he wanted, but nothing that he needed. He missed out on the true joy that comes from true Christian stewardship. He just couldn't let go of his stuff.

While I'm not sure stewardship looks the same for everyone, I'm convinced it's always about taking a much more holistic view of the Body of Christ. It's about seeing ourselves as we are—beloved children of the kingdom.

Application

1. Where are you on the consumer to steward continuum?

Consumer	Steward
• I believe God has called me to "subdue" the earth and "rule" over it	• I believe God has called me to weigh my wants against the needs of others—and use resources wisely
• I believe that ministry is a function of the church	• I believe ministry is everyone's responsibility
• I believe that church should meet my needs—and that of hurting people	• I believe I should help meet people's needs—through the church and as I have opportunity
• I believe other people would share our lifestyle and enjoy God's material blessings if they worked harder	• I believe in worshiping God by sharing the blessings I've been given

2. In what areas of your life have you been a consumer?

3. What would ministry look like in your world if stewardship became a guiding metaphor?

Retailer to Wholesaler

A Conversation about "Missions"

chapter 6

Have you seen the movie *A Christmas Story?* Nine-year-old Ralphie Parker wants one thing for Christmas: a genuine Red Ryder BB gun. From the moment he spies it in the window at the department store, it's his all-consuming passion. He talks about it, daydreams about it, writes essays about it. He even asks Santa for it.

To Ralph's dismay, every adult—including Mr. Claus himself—tells him the same thing: "You'll shoot your eye out!" By Christmas morning, the flannel-clad hero has all but given up hope. Then suddenly, he discovers one last present. Nervously, Ralph tears off the paper. His heart leaps. There it is! His beloved Red Ryder BB gun with "a compass in the stock and this thing which tells time!"

Now to be fair, I don't think I ever wanted a Red Ryder BB gun for Christmas. What I did want, however, was a camera. I was eleven at the time and—like Ralph—I was obsessed. Opening up the box on Christmas morning, I felt my jaw drop and my eyes light up. There it was: a genuine Kodak Instamatic! You would have thought my parents had bought me a brick of pure gold. I was so happy. Never mind that my new Instamatic was cheap and unsophisticated as cameras go. It was mine, all mine, and I was ecstatic to have it.

Almost immediately, I began running around the neighborhood taking pictures. Dogs, cats, fences, houses, trash cans—all were captured on film and transformed into works of photographic genius. Well, okay, maybe not genius, but I tried hard. It was fun experimenting with different angles and playing with shadows. Once I shot three rolls of film in a day—just for the pure joy of it.

Fortunately, for me, my mother approved of my new hobby. Pleased that I'd found something constructive to do with my time, she faithfully took me to the photo shop and worked hard to keep me in film and albums. Sometimes too, we'd stop off at the library so I could borrow resources on photography. The more I studied, the more I realized how much there was to know.

In junior high, my good fortune continued. Not only did my new school offer a photography class, they also had a real photographic darkroom. For the first time in my school career, I, Spencer Burke, found a class in which I could excel. And it wasn't a fluff course either.

The teacher, who had spent several years working as a professional photographer, was determined to make sure his students could find their way around a darkroom, inside and out. As a result, he was always doing things to keep us on our toes. One time he secretly switched up the chemicals, replacing the developing solution with vinegar. Another time he swapped out the bulb on the enlarger. By the end of the year, I'd learned to take nothing for granted. I'd check and double check everything, right down to the tiniest detail.

The photography learning curve continued in high school. Once again, I was blessed to have a wonderful teacher who knew his craft and challenged me to keep honing my technique. After a while, he encouraged me to start entering my pictures in competitions. When I was 15 years old, I entered a photo in the Kodak Scholastic National Photography Contest—and won.

Suddenly, I realized something. Photography was more than a fun hobby—it had the potential to be a career. If I could create some kind of unique brand that people liked, I could spend the rest of my life behind a camera. Inspired, that's exactly what I set out to do. Using prize money from competitions, I soon sported only the best equipment: Nikon bodies and lenses. With better equipment, I was able to garner more jobs, more recognition, more success. In 1977, I shot the cover of Chuck Colson's book, *Life Sentence*. A few years later, I was asked to do a photo shoot in Africa. After that, it was album covers.

It's funny. Colson, Africa—they were the kind of gigs photographers dream about. Yet, truth be known, I didn't find them all that enjoyable. There was a lot of pressure to perform. What had been simple as a kid somehow grew to become a complex science. Get it wrong—choose the wrong F-stop or select an unflattering angle—and I might be fired. Every day I had to constantly prove myself. I was really only as good as my last picture. In time, just keeping up with the latest photographic technology was a challenge.

So what's this story have to do with missions? A lot, actually. You see, what started out as a love became a burden. As the art of photography got increasingly complicated, my passion waned. In many ways, competition seemed to take the fun out of it. In my quest to be the best and to do things well, I somehow lost my joy. Eventually, I stopped taking pictures all together. When my last good camera broke, I decided not to buy another. I just hung up my flash and called it a day.

As I look at the church, I see a lot of burned out "photographers" sitting in the pews—people for whom the mission of the church has become a burden. They've grown weary of always trying to beat out their competitors for the choice assignments. They're tired of trying to have the latest and greatest gear and the best technique. After years of focusing on success, they seem to have lost sight of Jesus.

Target markets, strategic plans, statistical research—they're all part of what it means to do church in the modern world. How can we reach certain segments of the population? How can we be "relevant" to our culture? How can we get brand recognition in a crowded spiritual marketplace? The answer is almost always a cool new program or some kind of image overhaul. In many ways, we function like retailers—branding our goods, fending off the competition, and always trying to increase sales. The more success we find, the more success we actually need to keep it all going. We're photographers desperately trying to take the pictures we know people will buy.

In the past few years however, a new approach to missions has started to appear—one more suited, perhaps, to the postmodern culture. In this model, Christians see themselves not as retailers of the gospel, but as wholesalers of truth. Their main desire? Help people see the gospel in its raw beauty. No shrink-wrap, no free steak knives—just Jesus.

A few years ago I stopped into a little Mayberry-type general store while vacationing in Maine. On my way out, I noticed small disposable cameras for sale. With cardboard bodies and cheap plastic lenses, they hardly compared to the Nikons I'd once owned. Frankly, they hardly compared to my old Instamatic. Still, I was intrigued. I forked over the six bucks and got back into my car. The fall colors whizzed along out the window beside me. Suddenly I had an idea. Since the images from this camera were probably going to be blurry anyway, why not exaggerate the motion? What if I whipped my arm around while simultaneously clicking the shutter?

And so it was that I discovered "sling shots." Unhindered by bells, whistles, and all kinds of high-tech features, I re-discovered my passion. In breaking all the rules, I found something I thought I'd lost forever—the joy of taking pictures. Who would have thought that a blur could be so spectacular? And yet, somehow, it all worked.

In a sense, I followed Curly's advice in the movie *City Slickers*:

Curly: You know what the secret of life is?
Mitch: No, what?
Curly: This.
Mitch: Your finger?

Curly: One thing. Just one thing.
Mitch: That's great, but what's the one thing?
Curly: That's what you've got to figure out.

The following conversations pick up on this theme. What is the "one thing" when it comes to missions? What does it mean to move away from a retail mindset and instead function as a wholesaler? How has the obsession with packaging and branding affected the church?

Topic: Rant 2023-Tired of Cool

[Posted by: liquidthinking]

Maybe the greatest thing that could happen in the lives of the Bride is for the church buildings in America to be torn down. Break out the wrecking ball!

Can you say wake up call? I'm tired of churches trying to be hip, cool, and the next great thing. If I hear one more youth pastor say that church/Jesus should be cool, I'm going to throw up. Most fog machine blowing, disco-tech lighting, music playing, live band playing, goatee shaven, leather jacket wearing, candle lighting, video making, skit acting churches are more of the same stale barren excuse for the Bride.

I happen to like music, bands, lights, and candles, but not as a fresh sales pitch. Is it possible the reason most people don't know Jesus is because they've been to church?

Break out the wrecking ball? It sounds harsh, but do you hear his heart? Here's someone who's sick of the marketing and tired of the hype. You can see it, can't you? A guy walks into a church that sings, "It's All About You Jesus," but senses in his spirit that it's a lie. His stomach turns. It's not about Jesus at all. It's about fog machines and disco lighting. It sells, all right, but is it authentic?

[Posted by: footer]

What continues to amaze me is that the church really thinks that it's impressing the world with its cool stuff..."Gee Dick, the worship music has a good beat and I can dance to it...I think I'll rate them a 9.7 and come back here next week."

I remember seeing two TV shows in the past year that were very telling about church in our culture. One was an episode of Frasier where the female character talks about her car breaking down in front of a church just when the "show" was letting out—in reference to a worship service! And the other was an episode of Ed about a

---

small church's worship committee putting pressure on its pastor to be
more entertaining like the growing churches in town...only to find out
that people from the hip, cool, churches go to their (uncool) pastor
when they are in trouble because he really cares for people.

I think our culture sees us trying to be cool and sees our shallowness with it. I polled my kids at school—a Christian school—about
what church should be like.... Number one answer here in Tulsa? Fun.
What are we showing kids and people?

[Posted by: jsimmonds]

Liquid, I find myself agreeing with a lot of what you say. You
articulate your heart very well. But I'm more concerned about the
heart behind the expressions of church than about the actual methods. In my mind, if there's a guy up front with a clip-on tie
singing Maranatha praise songs from his heart as worship to the
Lord, I'm cool with that. If he meets in a building, great. If the
people in that body are loving God and loving people, right on. If
they're not—which some aren't—then that's a problem. Is it cheesy?
Maybe. Does the world look at it and make fun of it? Probably.
(But I think you'd agree that whether or not the world finds it
"relevant" doesn't matter.) Would I want to be a part of it? Nope.
But I'm not gonna ask a guy to take a wrecking ball to a place he
meets the Lord with his bro's and sis's in Christ.

[Posted by: footer]

What the heck makes everyone so nervous when we have discussions
about "tearing down," changing, or leaving the existing system of
church. It's like most everyone says, "Yeah, it's got a heck of a
lot of problems. Yeah, it's not what Christ probably intended. Yeah,
it uses and abuses people. Yeah, it's consumeristic and shallow. Yeah,
it's not really about Christ most of the time. But hey, don't talk
about changing it, don't talk about tearing it down. After all, it's
the Bride of Christ!"

Look, no one is talking about taking away brother John's place to
meet with Jesus and be changed by that relationship. No one is
talking about wrecking places where true community is happening. No
one is talking about throwing out the Bride with the dirty, stained,
filthy dress she sometimes wears. But when the dress is dirty,
please...please, someone get the woman a change of clothes!

We're like some freaking dysfunctional family that can't talk openly
about its problems and our need for change—problems that everyone
in the neighborhood sees (and talks about) whether we do or not. Do
we really think Jesus has a problem with us talking honestly about
the situation? How the heck—according to Barna—can FEWER than

1/3 of ALL REGULAR CHURCH GOERS say that they have EVER experienced God in their LIFETIME? What are we doing? And yet we defend it to the end. How long will we ignore what the world really sees in us: shallowness, greed, judgment, self-righteousness? For once, I would love to hear someone criticize Christians by saying, "Man, all they do is get out and help people. And they forgive too much! Some of those freaks are giving up everything to help others....My neighbor became a Christian and sold his lake house to feed some children somewhere. That church over there gave up the building project idea to build a homeless shelter/church instead.... They thought a new church building alone would be a waste of space since it's empty overnight."

I thought salvation and healing started with confession and repentance...and to me repentance is partly about in the words of Mike Knott—"knocking down everything I've tried to build, tossing out everything I tried to save." And so should it be with the church.

I've heard it said that non-profit organizations have lifecycles. When an organization begins, there's often tremendous optimism and hope. People's energies are focused on getting things done, moving ahead, and making a difference. Over time, however, the focus of the organization changes. At some point, the "building" phase comes to an end and the "maintenance" phase begins. Eventually, more energy gets directed toward keeping the organization alive than toward achieving the original objective.

Topic: Organized Crime/Religion...Whatever

[Posted by: JAK]

I think there are way too many people sitting in church services, year after year, getting absolutely nothing from the experience and yet somehow thinking this is OK. We never experience God in his awesome fullness. And so both God and we are ripped off. Something is wrong, and I place most of the blame on that thing our society calls "church."

I don't keep eating at a restaurant where the food sucks and I get sick after being there. Yet over and over, we expect people to be satisfied with our cultural expression of "church." We wonder why there is not much personal growth, or why our culture isn't being impacted by the Christian community.

The system is producing what it was designed to produce.

[Posted by: jugdish]

...it seems that a lot of churches, especially smaller congregations, are after numbers. They need money to grow so they are afraid to challenge people for fear that they will leave. The church has thrust itself into a maintenance mode, not doing anything to disrupt the status quo so that they do not lose the almighty tithe—and thus the ability to do "real ministry."

Many people leave because their needs are not being met. They're looking for meat in sermons/teachings and instead are being fed milk. Why are we so afraid to challenge people? Don't you think if people are growing then the church will grow, as well as the general fund?

[Posted by: tammy]

They're afraid to offend and lose people, because they run churches like businesses. As long as any incorporated church owns property, they will need to consider the business model when making decisions. Otherwise, they can't pay the bills. The problem lies in the way we have structured the thing we call church.

[Posted by: jugdish]

Herein lies a deeper issue with the church. If we're afraid to lose people—and their money—because we have bills to pay, where has our faith in God gone? Has the church lost Its trust that God will provide?!

Have we lost our passion? Many of these posts seem to suggest that we have—that maintenance of a system, and not the mission, has become our first priority. The next thread picks up on this theme.

Topic: Image, Hype, Church

[Posted by: soulrevolution]

Is it wrong for the church to present itself to today's culture in a way that is appealing and attractive? If we are arguing that the mere act of creating an image of church that is attractive to others is wrong, then what are we left with? More importantly, can we present an image of Jesus Christ that is both real and attractive?

[Posted by: liquidthinking]

Image is the consumer's greatest idol. Much of what we experience in our lives these days is not reality. The church that promotes itself to the public is all about image. Example: The church that averages 75 people in attendance, shoots a commercial to air on TV to promote a picnic. The video is shot at the largest event the church has ever had (say 200). There are shots of kids and parents smiling. Words flash: "Exciting! Relevant!" What you see on the commercial is not 100% who they really are. It is actually 50% really them, 25% what they were at one event, and 25% who they want to be. People see the commercial. They like the idea of an exciting and relevant church. So they go. The next week there are 200 people at the picnic. Why? Because the church created a pseudo-event. I like what Dennis Miller says: "Hype is the glittering rhinestone on the jumpsuit of mediocrity that catches our eye and makes us think, Hey maybe the Spice girls don't suck. It's the triumph of substance over style, predicated on the sad truth that most of us, if the gift-wrapping on the outside of the box is fancy enough, won't notice that inside there's nothing but a big pile of ----."

If there's one thing retailers are good at, it's packaging. The reality is pretty boxes and eye-catching displays sell products. The question is can we deliver what we promise? Or have we focused on the box to the exclusion of what's inside? Just what is it that we're selling anyway?

[Posted by: ken]

"Image is nothing. Thirst is everything. Obey your thirst." — Sprite Commercial

"Come, all you who are thirsty, come to the waters; and you who have no money, come, buy and eat! Come, buy wine and milk without money and without cost." — Isaiah

There is a distinct difference between appearing to be a relevant church and BEING a relevant church. It's interesting that Jesus and Paul put such an emphasis on ministry to the Body. On the night before Jesus' death, he tells the disciples, "By this all men will know that you are my disciples, if you love one another." He could have said, "if you love the Gentiles," or "if you love everyone" (that would have been much more palatable). But, instead, it seems Jesus wanted the disciples to love the other disciples! Well, that's pretty dumb, isn't it? Jesus certainly doesn't expect to win any converts inside the church, does He? What kind of growth plan is that, anyway? Okay, we're talking about cultural relevance, not church growth. But, still, he could have said, "if you are relevant." Instead, his thing was making sure the disciples loved each other (i.e., laid down their lives for each other).

I don't want to slam the desire to be relevant. I think we can get lost in the quest, though, and find ourselves forgetting that Christianity is trans-cultural and that love is always relevant to everyone, everywhere. What's more, part of the problem of modernity is that it systematizes everything, turning spiritual realities like love into programs, and interpersonal communication into broadcasts. By chasing a desire to be relevant, rather than love people, we're falling back into the modernity box!

Is it that the culture doesn't think they'll find anything meaningful in our congregations? Or, is it that they're right?

Topic: Is the church relevant to today's culture?

[Posted by: liquidthinking]

We like to make Jesus simple and put him in a fancy Pottery Barn box so we can sell him. But that is foolish. Even though our cool and hip GAP Jesus draws in the kids, we are selling Jesus short. Let's face it...it's far easier to sell Jesus than to actually know him. It's far easier to get people actively doing things for the false Jesus than creating space for people to meet the real Jesus. We spend far more time playing dress the Jesus doll, than actually being with the Father ourselves....When I dress Jesus up, I always end up tainting his true character.

As I read through these threads, I'm reminded of Jesus' words in Matthew 16:26, "What good will it be for a man if he gains the whole world, yet forfeits his soul?"

Topic: Ancient-Future Diversity

[Posted by: mr_magoo]

Until you stop asking how to become relevant, you will never be relevant. A monk in a cell isolated from the world becomes relevant, not when he puts on sunglasses and gets a gig with Letterman, but when the story he is living becomes important to the world at large. The more he is totally himself with God, the more relevant he becomes. In this way, the church becomes relevant by being more true to its ancient roots. This is why I love the ancient church people here on the ooze. I don't agree with their conclusions about what it means to be the ancient church, but I totally agree with their point that the next thing isn't supposed to be new and minty fresh.

We are not the purveyors of the new cool, but just a bunch of people trying to live for Jesus. The problem is that there was the "contemporary church" thing that started in the 1960s and the general assumption is that this postmodern thing is just "new contemporary."

[Posted by: DesertPastor]

The emerging ancient-future phenomenon is fascinating (Ancient-Future Faith, by Robert Webber is a must read). Many of the postmodern churches I've visited have included some ancient "feeling" components such as gothic-looking candles, Old Irish hymns, Celtic crosses, the practice of lectio divina, etc. Much of what is considered "ancient," however, has distinctly European roots. And so I'M WONDERING...will an ancient-future emphasis within postmodern worship undermine the cultural importance of racial diversity? Are there "other" ancient faith practices that will resonate with those of Asian, Hispanic, and African descent better than the more European ones?

Here's where the conversation takes a turn. Up until this point, the discussion has centered on ways we consciously package Christianity—that is, things we intentionally do to make the Christian message attractive. This post brings up the issue of unconscious packaging—that is, the cultural assumptions that become part and parcel of the gospel over time. How do we define church, for instance? Are six people meeting in a home a "church"—or just a small group? How has our geography and ethnicity affected our faith? Do we know where the gospel ends and cultural tradition begins?

[Posted by: Addai]

Yes, there are other ancient faiths that are more appropriate for ethnicities. There is a whole collage of Oriental Orthodox churches which would fit other ethnic groups more closely. This is actually an important point because some groups, like black Muslims, see Christianity as being a purely European (white) religion. The existence of the Coptic and Ethiopian churches, however, is proof they are wrong. My church has its roots in Asia, and successfully evangelized as far down as Japan at one time, and we think may have potentially reached the Philippines.

[Posted by: DesertPastor]

Learning what those "other" ancient faith traditions are—especially the non-European ones—is what occupies my thoughts most these days.

[Posted by: tammy]

I find it intriguing that there's an entire history of the early church which was not recorded as carefully as the one we are more familiar with. We have only a small percentage of the whole story. This has great impact on the thinking that we "need to return to the way the early church did things." Hmm.

As the North American/Western church, it's easy to assume that everyone does church like we do. And yet, as Addai points out, there is another Christian tradition that has been co-existing for centuries: Eastern Orthodoxy. I find this next post particularly fascinating. How far back are we willing to go in "unpackaging" our faith? Well, in Addai's case, right back to the apostles.

```
[Posted by: Addai]

The history may be more "fragmentary" in terms of written
records, because persecution against Christians was generally longer
lasting and more vicious.

While there may be less written records, that doesn't mean that
Church doesn't know what's going on. For instance, I can trace my
lines of consecration back to the original apostles like Jude, alias
Addai, and Barnabas (I forget his Aramaic name). This basically works
like a spiritual genealogy. So instead of saying this guy begat so
and so, I can say St. Addai and Bartholomew consecrated Mari, who
consecrated Mar Jacobus (who several pages later)...consecrated
Boltwood, who consecrated Bishop John (alias Mar Yokannon), who
consecrated me. How many folks do you know who can do this?
```

So what's the difference between retailers and wholesalers?

Retailers specialize in off-the-shelf, one-size-fits-all solutions. They give you all the pieces they think you need—plus complete instructions—all in one convenient package.

Wholesalers, on the other hand, don't worry about how pretty the box looks when they're selling to their customers. Often, they're providing raw goods—the ingredients for something else. They'll happily sell you large quantities of whatever it is you need and let you figure out what you're going to do with it all.

As I see it, the shift from retailer to wholesaler in missions is about letting go—stepping back and letting God build the kingdom.

As a youth pastor in the 1980s, I spent a lot of time trying to be "cool." I'd take kids to the amusement park or plan big water ski outings. I'd do anything, really, that I thought might attract kids. After all, that's what all the youth ministry books said to do. How did you connect with kids? You offered them lots of fun—and a little Jesus. Then one year I decided to try something different. I took a handful of kids on something called The Veneration Trek—A Journey in Worship. Parents thought I was crazy. "What?! You expect kids to go to a worship camp?" they asked with puzzled looks on their faces. But the truth was, it was the kids who'd given me the idea. When I asked them what they liked to do, they said things like, "Hang out with my friends and God and talk," or "Do stuff outside."

So that's what we did. We spent five days in Yosemite, just contemplating nature and listening for the voice of God. One morning, we all sat at the bottom of Half

Dome and I read through the creation account. Another day, we went hiking and did a mini silent retreat. At night, we'd sit around the campfire and talk or sing together. On the last day, we took communion. It was amazing.

Three years later, hardly anyone wanted to go water skiing anymore. They wanted to come out to The Veneration Trek instead. They didn't want just fun, they actually wanted to experience God. We had kids come out who'd never been to church before. I had kids come up and tell me they'd made decisions for Jesus Christ on the trip. It was crazy.

Had I stuck with a retail mindset, that trip never would have happened. It was the moment that I threw out my youth manuals and all the pre-packaged programs that things started to happen. Was Veneration Trek seeker-sensitive? Absolutely not. The whole thing was about worship. And yet, incredibly, it seemed like the less we tried to package the gospel and hide who we were, the more attractive we became. When we stopped trying to cloak Christianity in some kind of "culturally relevant" disguise, amazing things happened.

In missions, the retailing mindset shows up in all kinds of different ways. At times, we may be overly concerned with marketing—what do people want and how can we give it to them? We might go through a season where we focus on the upsell—how can we get people to become more committed, more loyal to our brand? At other times, our retailing behavior may be more subtle. We may insist that people who are new to the church go through a particular discipleship program. We might advocate one particular view of evangelism because it's "the biblical model." We might refuse to work with other churches because they don't share our exact theology. Or, we may insist on using a certain worship style or a certain type of leadership training. In every case, we're effectively adding something to the gospel.

It's trite, but retailers in missions major on the minors. As Liquid Thinking said in one of his posts, we start thinking that Jesus needs to be dressed up a little—maybe surfer shorts and a pair of Oakley sunglasses. The truth is we need to strip that stuff off him and get back to the basics of our faith.

When we have a wholesaler mindset, we're more inclined to trust that the story of Jesus Christ is powerful enough on its own. We tend to focus, not on how we can make ourselves look relevant, but how we can be relevant—through authentic life change. We live out the gospel in front of people and then let go, allowing the Holy Spirit to guide them into truth. As wholesalers, we share "the raw materials," and then give people the freedom to embrace them in their own way.

In Yosemite, I really didn't teach the kids. I didn't have formal lesson plans or fill-in-the-blank activity sheets. I really didn't have much of anything except faith—a faith that God would speak to individual hearts. It was missions without a net, really. And like sling shots, it was a wonderfully freeing experience.

Spiritual retailers, by nature, feel a pressure to make things happen. Somehow we think that if we can just package the gospel in a sexy enough box—or maybe find the right biblical proof texts—that people will come running. We're always trying to control every last detail. We develop and sell comprehensive programs because we want to make sure that people get it right—that nothing is left open to interpretation. Part A goes into Slot B and connects with Wire C. We not only want the world to buy our product, but also to use it the right way—following our rules and instructions.

A few years ago, my father came to visit us. One night, he decided to stay up and read while the rest of us went to bed. Some time later, I rolled over in bed and noticed motion in the living room. Looking through the window, I watched as my father got up out of his chair and reached for the X-10 controller. Now for those of you who aren't gadget people, an X-10 controller is a kind of central remote control for every electrical thing in your house. Lights. TVs. VCRs. You can operate all kinds of devices using the system. The Burke family actually has two of these gadgets. We keep one remote in the living room; the other in our bedroom.

When I saw my father reach for his controls, I decided to have some fun with mine. As he used his remote to turn the lights off, I used mine to turn them on. He tried again. The same thing happened. We went back and forth like this for several minutes. My father, an engineer by trade, was determined to figure the system out. There he was in boxer shorts and white socks, pacing back and forth in the living room, scratching his head. Finally, my wife let him in on the secret. "It's your son!" she yelled from the window.

Control is illusory. Even when we think we have it, we don't. We turn the light out. It comes back on. We try to beat the system through logic and careful planning. It doesn't work. We try new marketing gimmicks and revise our business plans—all to no avail. The light just keeps coming on. To many in the world, the modern church looks as silly as an old man in boxer shorts, waving a remote control.

In the church today, there's a desire to return to simpler days—to rediscover, as Curly says, "the one thing." Adopting the wholesaler mindset gives us a chance to start over—to move beyond exporting a program, release people into the Holy Spirit's care, and allow God to be responsible for building the kingdom.

Application

1. Where are you on the continuum between retailer and wholesaler?

Retailer	Wholesaler
• I believe we need to make the gospel message more attractive for today's culture	• I believe the gospel is attractive to people in every culture
• I believe it's important to give people "a complete package"	• I think it's okay to give people raw goods
• I see other stores/other brands as a threat	• I believe in distributing goods so that other businesses can succeed

2. In what ways have you packaged the gospel or tried to control other people?

3. What might wholesale missions look like in your context? What's holding you back?

Adversary to
Ally

A Conversation about "Faith"

Chapter 7

I've sat through more than my fair share of traffic jams over the years. Big ones, little ones, and lots of in-between ones. Needless to say, I've also seen plenty of car ornaments in my time, including a fascinating assortment of fish symbols. Let's see…there's the Jesus fish, the fish with legs, the fish with legs getting eaten by the Jesus fish, the fish with Greek text, the fish with "Darwin" written in it, and of course, your basic all-purpose Ichthus. I hate to admit this, but I actually had several of these items on my own car at one point. In fact, back in the 1970s, my car was virtually held together with Jesus bumper stickers.

My first car was a 1967 Plymouth Valiant. With a slant six engine and a "Slide over, Baby," bench seat, it was everything a 17-year-old kid could want—and then some. In an earlier life, the vehicle had actually been used to deliver blueprints for my father's business. By the time I inherited it, however, it had been in several accidents. With a passenger door that had to be lassoed shut and a window that regularly rolled down by itself, it was quite a sight. Nevertheless, that old car got me around. What's more, it gave me a perfect platform to declare my faith.

I can't really remember the first sticker I bought for it. Was it "Smile Jesus loves you!" or "Jesus is coming back and boy is he mad!"? Well, in any case, by the time I was graduated from high school, the car was tattooed with religious sentiments. Getting honked at was a way of life for me. And of course, whenever people would yell or make rude gestures, I'd inevitably assume it was because God was dealing with their hearts—you know, convicting them through my stickers. Did it ever occur to me that maybe I was a bad driver? Or that perhaps I'd just stolen someone's parking spot? Not a chance.

In 1977, however, my perspective began to change. I was living in Berkeley at a Christian commune called Dwight House. Open to people on spiritual sojourns, Dwight House was well known for its hospitality. It was a safe place to crash and to converse. Each night, we'd hang out with each other. New people were always joining us—sometimes just for dinner, sometimes for a few days. I'd been there a couple of months when the topic of my stickers came up. "Are you more interested in telling people what you believe or hearing what they have to say?" a house mate named Alan asked. My jaw dropped. I hedged. "Well, um…." Busted. I can still remember going down to the car and feverishly trying to scrape the stickers off.

Let's be honest. Very few people who saw all my Jesus paraphernalia felt anything but resentment. My stickers were an irritant to other Christians and downright inflammatory to most everyone else. I put them there, not for other people's benefit, but for my own. I wanted the world to know who I was and what I stood for. Had I been born about 2,000 years earlier, I no doubt would have skipped bumper stickers and gone right to long tassels. I wouldn't have had, "Praise the Lord God!" plastered on my car, but rather on my forehead—inside a wonderfully wide phylactery. After all, that's what the Pharisees did (Matthew 23:5).

At that particular time in my life, I lived in a very black and white world. I needed to know who was in and who was out; who was an adversary and who was an ally. The fish sign, of course, reportedly started out for exactly that purpose. When the earliest followers of Jesus were persecuted and forced to worship in hidden locations, they would scratch the secret symbol of a fish in the ground to help them identify their brothers and sisters. It was a secret handshake of sorts.

But as I learned that summer at the commune, even the fish handshake wasn't always reliable. I lived with "Christians" at the commune, but many of them didn't look anything like the people I had grown up with. Some of them smoked. Others drank. I remember the first weekend they asked me if I wanted to go to church. Of course I said yes. They told me to go upstairs at 10:00 A.M. Sunday. Cool, I thought. We'll meet together, hop in someone's car and head downtown. Imagine my surprise when we didn't end up going anywhere, but instead served each other communion at home. Their "church" was a house church! The congregation was the same bunch of scraggly people I'd eaten stale bagels with the night before at dinner. How could this be? There were no greeters, no ushers, no Sunday school teachers. What kind of church was this?

My time in the commune taught me a lot of things. It forced me to reexamine many of the walls I had put up between myself and other people. Having grown up in a town that made the folks in *Footloose* look liberal, I found living in Berkeley to be a massive adjustment in and of itself. Add in the diversity I found at the commune and my worldview was soon stretched in all kinds of wonderful ways. I went to dinner with the Moonies. I sat in on lectures with Elisabeth Kubler-Ross. I photographed Tibetan lamas. I even watched Uri Geller bend spoons.

I was exposed to all kinds of different conversations that year and found it incredibly stimulating. Not only was I able to be salt, light, and a sweet aroma, but I also learned a great deal from these people. Talking with the "adversary"—all the people who didn't have fish on their cars—proved to be a great boon to my faith.

As I look at the church today, I see a similar shift taking place. People are beginning to question many of the walls that have existed between Christians and the world. Adversaries, in many cases, are becoming allies. Is it possible, for instance, that we have more in common with "secular people" and other religious groups than we realize? Could we find value in talking to these people apart from evangelistic endeavors? What about our relationship with other denominations? How important is it to keep sparring over things like baptism, predestination, and eschatology? What about the age-old Catholic/Protestant split?

Here's what I've been hearing at TheOoze:

Topic: "Christian" Enterprises

[Posted by: Galadriel]

What do you all think about stores, books, bands, businesses, etc., that market themselves as a "Christian" store, book, band, business, etc.?

[Posted by: robgraham]

Good question!!! But, don't you get it? The christening is our protection from the "big bad world." I mean, aren't all the non-Christian business people out to rip me off and the Christian business people are only looking out for me and not themselves? Don't we need to be able to identify who is our brother "out there"? After all, I'd hate to see our incredible unity suffer because we couldn't identify one another properly. Personally, I'm in favor of Christian name badges. The Christian business thing was cool, but hey, when I go in 7-11 I have NO idea WHO I'm dealing with! Those name badges could come in real handy. In fact, we need not only the "Christian" Yellow Pages, we need the "Christian" White Pages. Think of it! You could dial anyone in the directory and they would be true, honest, just, pure, folks. Wow!

How do we interact with the world? That's really what the shift from adversary to ally is about. Given that we already have Christian TV channels, amusement parks, and awards shows, maybe buying Slurpees from the "saved" isn't so far off. Or is it? Why are we so suspicious of anyone who doesn't look, sound, or smell like we do?

[Posted by: dwight]

I think only people are Christians. A business may be Christian owned, but the business is not Christian. A band may be a little

---

different since the members could all be Christians. A bookstore can sell books by Christians for Christians, but the store itself is not Christian. All the Christian labeling is a good example of Constantinianism. He initiated the "Christening" of institutions.

[Posted by: jsimmonds]

robgraham is touching on the issue beneath the issue: fear. I'm reading a book right now by John Fischer called Fearless Faith. He argues that the whole Christian marketing thing is driven by fear.

I tend to agree. What do you all think?

[Posted by: Galadriel]

I've never read Fischer's book, but his thesis makes sense to me. Christians, like many people, are often afraid of things they don't understand or agree with.

Many products and services advertised today use fear to convince us that we need them. The only real difference between "Christian" and "secular" products that do this is WHAT they teach us to fear.

[Posted by: jsimmonds]

The essence of the fear is that Christians are scared of being polluted by the world. This is reflected in Christian music (marketed heavily to Christians and not the rest of the world), the construction of church buildings, Christian T-shirts, the whole nine yards. Fear of making contact with the real world (and thus being screwed up by it) drives a lot of these things.

Fischer's book is built around John 17:3. Jesus prays that we would not be taken from the world (Fischer says we've taken ourselves out and become our own subculture), but instead be protected from the evil one.

[Posted by: bigdrink]

J, I haven't read the book, but I saw the movie. It starred this kid in glasses with a lightening shaped scar on his forehead whose mom and dad died because they gave up their lives for him. He lived under a staircase and was hated by his guardians. When his biography was supposed to be on A&E, the Christians got together to picket....Wait, it was the news and Harry Potter is the Antichrist. I think that fear motivated that whole show of solidarity.

It's true. The Christian subculture thrives, in part, because of fear. Believing that the world is an evil place to raise our children, we take a variety of steps to insulate ourselves from that reality. We watch Christian videos, read Christian books, and listen to Christian music. Why? Because we deem these items to be "safe." When Harry Potter mania swept the world, many felt compelled to stand against it. Not only were Harry Potter titles not published by a Christian publishing house, they contained magic and sorcery. A story of good versus evil perhaps, but what if children misunderstood? At least C.S. Lewis and J.R. Tolkien had Christ-figures. And so Harry Potter was added to the black list. Parents picketed and pastors preached. Meanwhile, the world around us took it all in.

Thread: Reasons People Leave Church

[Posted by: johnmccollum]

I think our church has driven away many people—especially those in emerging generations with its failure to articulate a compelling vision of what it is we stand for and where it is we're going. It's not that we soft-pedal our theology we are very committed to the authority of Scripture. It's just that we spend so much time defining what we're NOT about. And what we're AGAINST. But it's difficult to determine what we're FOR.

We're against abortion and promiscuity and false teaching and everything a church is supposed to be against. But it's so much more difficult to craft a positive, proactive mission. Like one that embraces and passionately pursues opportunities to dispense mercy and exhibit self-sacrifice along with a meaningful commitment to meeting the physical, spiritual, and educational needs of our neighbors.

This next thread explores the idea of inter-faith dialogue. How do we approach people from other religions? Do we see them as adversaries—or potential allies?

Topic: Many Voices, One God

[Posted by: Madison58]

The second tenet of Progressive Christianity is: We are Christians who recognize the faithfulness of other people who have other names for the gateway to God's realm.

Often, any discussion of interfaith relations revolves around the desire to make contacts and introduce lost people to Christianity.

Sometimes there is an effort to find commonalities so that cooperative ventures can be executed, like food banks and shelters.

Another way is, "learning to like the others in their otherness. We might even indulge in a bit of 'holy envy.' That is, we see something beautiful in what is different from us, something highly desirable, instead of trying to find ways in which we are the same. If we can give up our ethnocentric view of the universe, we might learn that religious diversity is something we all need in order to realize our full potential as human beings."

[Posted by: preachinjesus]

---QUOTED---
The second tenet of Progressive Christianity is: We are Christians who recognize the faithfulness of other people who have other names for the gateway to God's realm.
---END QUOTE---

This is pretty much straight-up inclusivism, which I believe borders dangerously close to universalism. Inclusivism, as with universalism, is wrong. There is only one way to Heaven, that is Jesus Christ. None can be saved by any other religion or faith practice (i.e., Hinduism, Taoism, Hare Krishna, Islam, etc.) so I must ask what would it credit the Christian to take bits and pieces from other religions that are non-Christian and/or anti-Christian to attempt to reinforce one's personal faith? Sounds like that type of a person either (a) doesn't read the Bible all that much, (b) hasn't completely experienced the blessing and complete fulfillment of the Holy Spirit, or c) hasn't looked at the complete picture of Christianity to learn from its heroes, scholars, and leaders. (Note: I am not accusing anyone on this board of that, simply explaining things.) Christianity is the only complete faith based system available in the world and offers everyone who believes and is saved the complete religious experience.

Our potential as human beings is fulfilled when we accept Jesus Christ as Lord and Savior of our lives and that potential continues to be built up as we make disciples among the nations and neighbors.

It's interesting how willing we've been to entertain—and even embrace—a variety of "secular" viewpoints on things like art, literature, mathematics, politics, business, medicine, etc. over the years, but not spirituality. If someone is outside Christianity or even outside our particular theology, our tendency is to immediately shut down. Often we don't even leave ourselves the option of respectfully disagreeing. Instead, we just refuse to start the conversation.

Growing up, for instance, I was taught to steer clear of Catholics, Seventh Day Adventists, and Southern Baptists. Why? Because according to the "experts" in my world, these groups believed in "Jesus plus"—that is, faith in Jesus plus some other requirement to gain salvation. Consequently, a relationship with these people was out of the question. In an effort to avoid "the bad," I also missed out on "the good" these people had to offer.

[Posted by: Madison58]

My earlier quote was from Krister Stendahl, who has served as a Lutheran bishop in Sweden and as dean of the Harvard Divinity School. He recently pointed out to a seminar on interfaith solidarity the condescending nature of many attempts at starting conversation with people of other religions. He said that looking for similarities is "a dead end street." The message conveyed is that I can like you because you're more like me than I once thought.

"At present, most of us do not have the language to deal with the experience of plurality. Even to insist that 'authentic religion' has to be about God or a God, would shut many of the world's people out of the conversation. From what I have heard, many people in the East have no conception of our western notion of God, but these [the religion of these people] Christians tend to dismiss as 'idolatry.' We are hardly being respectful of all our neighbors when we insist that authentic religion requires a concept of God that is similar to the ones held by Jews, Muslims, and Christians."

Isn't it possible that becoming acquainted with the spirituality of a Buddhist might make us better Christians?

[Posted by: mr_magoo]

I both agree and disagree.

---QUOTED---
We are hardly being respectful of all our neighbors when we insist that authentic religion requires a concept of God that is similar to the ones held by Jews, Muslims, and Christians.
---END QUOTE---

We are hardly being respectful of God if we ignore his words about who he is. I personally would rather be respectful of the guy who created me from dust and could return me to dust in an instant.

But we have used that as an excuse in the past to distance and separate us from people who we don't agree with. I think there is a position that is respectful to God and is open to learning from other religions. But for me it doesn't start with "respecting people" as my highest value.

Magoo's position is a common one in the church today. There's a sense that shunning/ignoring other religious viewpoints is wrong, and yet a cautiousness about swinging the pendulum too far the other way as well. While there's a desire not to carry on as adversaries, it's uncertain what being an ally—and a follower of Jesus—would look like.

[Posted by: ultraman]

---QUOTED---
Isn't it possible that becoming acquainted with the spirituality of a Buddhist might make us better Christians?
---END QUOTE---

I think any knowledge is useful in helping us becoming better people, and better Christians too. I guess, though, I'm not sure what a better Christian looks like. There's a lot of stuff about Buddhism that is admirable. The Dalai Lama is one of my heroes. How can you not be inspired by one dedicated to performing acts of compassion for all the sentient beings in the universe? Sometimes I wish I knew of some Christians who were as "Christ-like" as he. But I have been to Tibet, and I have spent more time delving into Tibetan Buddhism than the average layman, and I can tell you, much as it pains me to say this, that it is quite demonic at its roots. And I am not one to use the demon word easily. Admittedly, Tibetan Buddism can be argued to be a warped version of Siddhartha'a original philosophy, but most practicing Buddhists see it as the purest expression.

This next thread picks up on potential conflicts within the Church. How do we see each other—as adversaries or allies? How is postmodernism affecting theology?

Topic: Is there a balance you Calvinists?

[Posted by: drumboy33]

I have many Calvinist friends who live and die by their "five points," but I refuse to encapsulate God with labels. I agree whole-heartedly that we are depraved; we need God. Time and time again in the Word, the authors tell us that "anyone who calls" on God will be saved (Romans 10:9, 13). Although God is that source, we still have that responsibility on our shoulders. Could there be a balance somewhere in our own asking and God's prompting or nudging? I say yes! Was my salvation predetermined in the courts of heaven? No! It was determined and finalized when I confessed with my own mouth, "God save me! I'm lost without you." I'm not saying that our salvation is completely on our shoulders, but I am urging you to think about this possible dual-origination between both us and God. I can't explain the trinity but I believe it. Preach your "tulip," but don't forget that they are people and have to make a decision themselves. Your theology looks good on paper, but to say man has no choice is against Scripture. Could there be a balance?

[Posted by: liquidthinking]

Your friends are partially right. And so are you. :-)

[Posted by: ezekiel]

I believe in both and then some....

For some who believe that God is all over their predestination into the kingdom...then perhaps they are right. One look at Paul and you see a guy who initially wasn't a willing participant.

For some who believe that God has given them (and everyone else) a wide open choice to join the party...then I believe God will not deny them. He will confess fathership over those who call him Father. The Bible supports this too.

God calls who He calls & chooses who He chooses—and is willing that none perish.

So maybe it's both in balance.

Calvinist & Hobbs

[Posted by: tammy]

What does TULIP stand for?

[Posted by: preachinjesus]

Tulip is actually an American seminary student's explanation of Calvinism. Pretty funny. I think he made it up for a test (supposedly) and it stuck.

Here it is...

1. T—Total depravity: Humans are sinful in nature and can do nothing to inherit eternal life in Heaven on their own account.

2. U—Unconditional Election: Humans are selected to be saved by God before the beginning of time.

3. L—Limited Atonement: God's election is only for a select group of people, the predestined elect in Christ.

4. I—Irresistible Grace: The call of God is so strong that no one can deny His call on their lives.

5. P—Perseverance of the Saints: Basically eternal security. Because God has chosen you before time to be saved, nobody can do anything to release you from His grip...even you.

I agree with a lot of the points of Calvinism, although I would heavily contest that Calvin held all five beliefs as they are stated above. Most of the beliefs of Calvinists come from the Synod of Dort where they confronted Jacobus Arminius...but enough on the church history stuff.

I am not a five-point Calvinist, though I believe you can prove all five points through Scripture and it is a whole lot more theologically sound than some of this other crap that people are serving up and calling theology. I digress.

I'd love to chat about this further. I consider myself a 3.5 point Calvinist, if you let me define the points properly.

Peace, love, and keep Jesus First,

[PreachinJesus]

P.S. The Arminians have DAISY: He loves me, He loves me not, He loves me, etc.

[Posted by: tammy]

Could we have both tulips and daisies in our garden? Can tulips and daisies co-exist, theologically speaking? I know they grow very well together in my backyard....

What?! Tulips and daisies in the same garden? 3.5 point Calvinism? Don't miss the significance of these comments. The impact of theology on postmodernism can't be overstated. This conversation would not have happened a generation ago. But increasingly, people are no longer comfortable coloring within the lines of traditional theology. Instead, they're picking and choosing the elements they feel create the most compelling theological picture—one that matches their particular reading of Scripture.

While the modern world would demand that one profess either Calvinism or Arminianism, the postmodern world seems to be able to accommodate bizarre new creations. One can be a Calvinist in the present reality and not spell anything. One can be a Calvminian or even a Presbycostal. However, as the next thread points out, under stress, our old habits die hard. We instinctively retreat to our old stomping grounds.

```
[Posted by: liquidthinking]

I'm sorta amazed at how we can play on these topics and be open
to new ideas with them...then quickly run back our theological
fortresses on this issue.

On one side is the predestination fortress.
On the other side the freewill fortress.
Both are wrong. Both are right.

But the minute you start defending a theology is the minute you
stop seeking truth.

So get out your white flags.

Come out and play with an open mind and let's figure out new
words to describe what God is up to, because frankly I'm tired of
both sides. I'm hoping to seek the truth. But if I have to choose
between these two options...then I'm not interested.

It's amazing to me how many of us talk about the hang ups and
downfalls of doctrinal constructs, and how they fall short of the
reality of who God is and how he works...only to see us rally behind
hard-line doctrine that is built upon modern concepts.

So, anyone game? Is there anyone left here to play a new game?
```

Shifting our mindset from adversary to ally means giving up an "us vs. them" orientation to the world around us. It means easing up on our boundaries and engaging people in conversation, not combat. It means being humble enough to let go of our prejudices and listen to other perspectives. Will we have differences? Of course. But unlike the modern world, those differences no longer need to keep us isolated from each other. We can agree to disagree, yet still be in relationship with each other—learning and growing together.

It's funny. Lots of people have asked me about TheOoze name over the past five years. What does it mean? Quite simply, I think it captures the new reality of the church. The church today is becoming increasingly ooze-y. As the old frameworks and structures are removed, we're coming together in new and wonderful ways. We're becoming much more fluid—rolling together at some points and rolling away again at others. Our shape is constantly changing.

In the postmodern world, the focus is on finding common touchpoints—with our culture, with other religions, and with each other. It's a significant switch for many of us. We're much more accustomed to rallying around flashpoints—hot button issues that demand a response. True to our Protestant roots, we've become more famous for what we're against than what we are for.

When I was a kid, I practically lived on hotdogs and hamburgers. A good old American boy, I didn't like to eat anything that wasn't made in the U.S.A. My poor parents. For years, my finicky tastes kept them out of all kinds of restaurants. One night my father decided he'd had enough. Off to the Mexican restaurant we went. And where was I? That's right, I stayed in the car. Although I'd never had Mexican food before, I was convinced I wouldn't like it. "Fine," said my Dad, closing the door. "Stay here." Of course, about a half hour into it, I weakened. Cold and hungry, I sheepishly wandered into the restaurant to join the rest of my family. I started off slow, of course. Just chips and salsa at first. On subsequent visits, I branched out and tried tacos and burritos. Eventually, Mexican dishes became some of my favorite foods. These days, it seems I have some sort of Mexican concoction at least once a week.

I mention that story because it seems to me that many of us are finicky eaters when it comes to our spirituality. In our defiant blindness, we've determined that we'd rather stay in the car or picket the restaurant than risk being in relationship with people who are different than we are. Now I'm not suggesting that we have to gorge ourselves on everything that's out there, but there is something to be said for living in community with other people. It's important to know where other people are coming from and to appreciate and embrace truth wherever it is found.

In my own life, I've found truth in some unlikely sources outside my immediate tradition. A few years ago, a silent retreat hosted by Brennan Manning introduced me to some of the riches of the Catholic Church. At the time, contemplation and spiritual direction were foreign concepts to me and yet, like Mexican food, they've since become a cherished part of my life. Those few days I spent with Brennan were absolutely life changing. I left the monastery aware not only that God loved me, but that he liked me. Years of head knowledge somehow moved down that weekend—into the most vulnerable, needy places of my heart.

In Hawaii, I remember visiting a bookstore and stumbling upon a book by Thomas Merton. Once again, I was struck by the incredible wisdom that could be found apart from the "approved" evangelical reading list. A Trappist monk, Merton gave me a new appreciation for the meaning of community. His *The New Man* and *New Seeds of Contemplation* touched my heart in ways other religious books had not.

Not long afterward, my thinking was stretched again, this time by Thich Nhat Hanh—a Buddhist monk who lived in Vietnam during the war. When his monastery was destroyed, he decided not to return to monastic life and instead help heal and care for his people. Instead of revenge and hate, Hanh dedicated his life to non-violence. In fact, Martin Luther King, Jr. once nominated Hahn for the Nobel Peace Prize. Hanh's *Living Buddha, Living Christ* gave me insight into Jesus from an eastern perspective. His thoughts on the incarnation seemed to fill in the gaps for me and help me appreciate God's redemptive plan in a fresh, vibrant way.

Then there were the people I met at the commune. One woman in particular stands out in my mind. In a wheelchair and suffering from Multiple Sclerosis, she joined us one evening for dinner. A know-it-all 19-year-old, I noted her obvious physical handicaps and assumed she was lacking mental function as well. Speaking was obviously a great effort for her and I found it hard to understand much of what she said. As the evening wore on, I quickly wrote her off. It was only when she left and I learned more about her background that I came to see how much I had missed in my arrogance. This woman had two Ph.D. degrees, had completed all kinds of amazing research projects, and was—bar none—a truly brilliant mind. Had I stopped to really listen to her, and somehow seen past my initial prejudice, I would have come away much the richer.

As I think back over these experiences, I can't help but wonder how many other opportunities I've missed along the way by choosing to "sit in the car." In Matthew 12:30, Jesus says, "He who is not with me is against me." While I believe separation can be a biblical principle, I can't help but think that I've overdosed on it. After all, in Mark 9:39, Jesus also says, "whoever is not against us is for us." Maybe we need to focus in on this verse for the next century or two. Who knows? We might find that some people who appeared to be adversaries are in fact allies.

For years, we've focused on excluding those people who don't appear to be for us. We've stiff-armed people, even other Christians. We've divided and subdivided and then divided again. In a sense, we've done the opposite of what Jesus advised in the Parable of the Weeds. When the disciples asked him if they should pull the weeds that seemed to be forming alongside the wheat, Jesus said no "because while you are pulling the weeds, you may root up the wheat with them. Let both grow together until the harvest" (Matthew 13:29–30).

Postmodernism offers us a chance to take Jesus' words literally—and to realize how interconnected and dependent we really are. As long as we are in these mortal bodies, walking on planet Earth, we're all in the same garden. We share the same soil and struggles. We're all on a quest for truth.

Will the weeds be ignored forever? Of course not. But Jesus says it's not our job to pull them out. So let's stop fighting each other and allow God to be God. Our task? To be rooted and established in love—growing and learning from each other.

Application

1. Where are you on the adversary to ally continuum?

<table>
<tr><td align="center">Adversary</td><td align="center">Ally</td></tr>
<tr><td valign="top">

- I am at odds with the world, other religions, and sometimes even other Christians
- I believe it is important to come out and be separate
- I believe in uniting only with people who share my particular theological perspective
- I believe truth is primarily found in one source: my interpretation of the Bible

</td><td valign="top">

- I think we have a lot in common with other people—after all, we're all sinners
- I believe it is important to journey together and focus on things we have in common
- I want to connect with others (no matter what they believe) and learn whatever truth I can from them
- I believe all truth is God's truth wherever it is found

</td></tr>
</table>

2. Can you think of a time when you "sat in the car," or isolated yourself, only to find out later what you were missing?

3. How would your life change if you were to see others as allies more than adversaries? What does it mean to be "in the world and not of it"?

Warrior to Gardener
A Conversation about "Evangelism"

Chapter 8

In high school, it seems like everyone has a claim to fame. Some people are known for their athletic abilities, some for their academic accomplishments, and still others for their artistic/musical genius. Of course, in the middle of that crowd, there are kids whose talents are less universally recognized. The girl who can blow a bubble as big as her head. Or the guy who can stick his arm up the vending machine without getting it stuck.

In my case, I was the crusading Christian—the guy who got Keith Green to come sing at our school. I not only mastered the Four Laws, I could give a solid gospel presentation in five minutes or less. Eager to do God's work, I regularly invited friends to church with me and rejoiced as they walked the aisle, prayed the prayer, and kneeled to receive Jesus Christ.

The older I grew, the bolder I became. When I co-founded my high school's closed circuit television channel, I did everything I could to get Jesus in there. I even listed him next to my name in the credits: "Directed by Spencer Burke—with special thanks to Jesus Christ."

In time, I stopped focusing my evangelism efforts on only those people I knew and instead began trying to convert complete strangers. The "I Found It" campaign was a particularly exciting time in my life. I remember dividing up the phone book, making cold calls and inviting person after person to come join our ranks. My friends even had a contest to see who could bring the most new members each month.

When someone accepted the offer I made—"Does this prayer express the desire of your heart?"—I was pumped and eager to go make the sale with someone else. When people rejected my plea, I never thought to find out why or what might be going on in their lives. To me, they were clearly destined for hell, beyond my help and out of God's reach—or so I thought. No point in beating my head against a wall. After all, there were lots of other people out there who needed Jesus.

Youth group was a big part of my high school experience. But even in junior high, I was already heavily involved in leadership. Knowing lots of kids from church gave me a certain confidence and popularity. In fact, by the end of junior high, I was voted student body president. But even though I knew a lot of people, I had few close friendships.

The transition from junior high to high school was tough. Certifiably cool in ninth grade, I was shocked to find myself sitting alone the next fall at high school. I remember one lunch hour in particular. The morning mist had turned to drizzle and the sky was threatening a real downpour. I was cold, lonely, and miserable. When Mr. Botello walked by I didn't think much of it. But then he spoke to me. Seeing my saddened face and soggy brown bag, he called me by name and invited me inside. I quickly grabbed my backpack and followed him to his classroom. A lowly freshman, I soon found myself shooting paper hoops with a bunch of upperclassmen. Grateful didn't even begin to cover it.

Ray Botello was widely regarded as one of the best teachers at the school. What's more, he taught photography, something that was quickly becoming a passion of mine. Our lunch that day birthed a strong friendship between us. Bit by bit, Ray shared his knowledge with me and encouraged me in the craft. Between football games, clubs, girls, and Jesus, I had a busy four years. Then at the end of my senior year, I was asked to deliver the final graduation speech. It was a Christian crusader's dream come true: "Class of 1977, you may now turn your tassels—and remember, Jesus loves you!"

Looking back, there's no question in my mind that I was a committed soldier in God's army. Throughout my high school career, I was passionate in my desire to see others come to Jesus Christ. I trained hard, armed myself with the right verses, and aggressively seized opportunities to share my faith. The only problem is I'm not sure being a Christian soldier was such a great thing—and it's even more problematic today.

For years, the warrior metaphor has permeated the Christian subculture, particularly our approach to evangelism. Take the Salvation Army. Or Campus Crusade for Christ. I don't know about you, but I grew up singing "Onward Christian Soldiers" and the "Battle Hymn of the Republic" on Sunday mornings. I did "sword drills" in Sunday school and played with cardboard cutouts of spiritual armor. In more recent years, a whole new crop of warrior songs has been written. Want a revival like the one in Pensacola, Florida? Better start singing "Enemy's Camp" on Sunday mornings and don't forget the motions. Where's the enemy? "He's under my feet!!" [stomp, stomp].

Now there's no question that the Bible is filled with war imagery, particularly in the Old Testament. But the Old and New Testament authors use a lot of other images—

including many earthy, agricultural pictures. While one still sees warrior language in Paul's writings, Jesus seems to be more partial to farmers, shepherds, and fishermen. Taking the ground by force just didn't seem to be in his nature.

Back in 1977, I was too young and in too much of a hurry to really appreciate all that Ray contributed to my life. And yet, the more I reflect on those years, the more I realize that he was a powerful missionary. Did he ever invite me to his church? Not that I remember. Did he ever extol me to explore my relationship with Jesus Christ in a deeper or different way? Never. In fact, I don't think we ever really discussed religion. Still, Ray looked an awful lot like Jesus to me. He stood by me in good times and bad. He nurtured and guided me. His trust and friendship were steadfast.

In many ways, Ray was a spiritual gardener. He planted seeds in kids and let God grow them to maturity. While I felt pressure as a Christian to produce instant results and claim spiritual territory, Ray seemed content to wait on a harvest. He seemed to understand that living out your faith is often more important than preaching it. Every day, Ray walked the walk. He didn't need to persuade anyone of the grace and goodness of God. He lived it.

The difference between warriors and gardeners is significant. Warriors take territory by force; gardeners faithfully till and water the soil. While warriors are busy attacking, gardeners plant and fertilize.

Then there's the matter of seasons. While warriors press on no matter what the elements, gardeners step back on occasion. They know that working the soil incessantly leads to burnout. They understand the importance of rest—of allowing a field to lie fallow for a year in order to regenerate itself. At the same time, however, they're also keenly aware of the mystery of spiritual growth. Spiritual gardening is not an exact science. While gardeners faithfully do their part, they experience peace knowing that God is ultimately responsible for the crop.

The fact is the established church has been on the warpath non-stop for decades. People have heard sermon after sermon about seizing opportunities. They've gone to seminar after seminar on how to win friends and influence people—for Jesus. They've bought videos, listened to tapes, and filled in workbooks. And yet, like me, they've watched as many of the people they so faithfully led to Jesus Christ have wandered away from the church. Why?

After years in the battle, many warrior Christians have become discouraged. Deep down, they wonder if they ever understood "the gospel." If Jesus is such good news, why do they feel so down—so completely exhausted—by the thought of telling others about him? Why isn't it "working" for them anymore?

The church today is struggling to come to a new understanding of evangelism. They're weary of the old paradigms and eager for fresh insight. Still, the process is a scary one. If the gospel isn't simply The Four Laws, what is it?

Topic: Define 'gospel'

[Posted by: rickwell]

What is "the gospel" to you? If/when you share it with others, what is it?

That's the "simple" question. As I feel compelled to lead people to Jesus and share with them the hope that is in me, what am I sharing? Is it the 4 Spiritual Laws? Is it the Romans Road?

[Posted by: fess2]

It is neither of those....The gospel is basically good news. You give a testimony to what God has done. You share how you got saved and ultimately how you were before you became saved. But don't dwell on this, otherwise it glorifies the sin and sinful nature. It's a pet peeve of mine when people spend 30 minutes on drugs, sex, and prostitutes and only two minutes on "Then I became saved." Spend time on how you became saved whether using Romans Road, The Four Spiritual Laws, Colors, Peace treaty, etc. Share your story and then finally tell what God is doing in your life now. The gospel is just that: good news that God came, saved, and wants us to love him and to love others....

[Posted by: liquidthinking]

The 4 Spiritual Laws are stupid.
Tracts are stupid.
Stop using them.

"The kingdom of God is at hand"—Jesus

That's the gospel.

The problem with far too many churches is that they are filled with people (and some leaders???) who do not know what the gospel is. The gospel leads to loving others. It leads to a life of service. Yet our church buildings are filled with people who are there for them-selves because they love only themselves.

Frankly, if it's good news I'll tell people about it. If it's not, I won't. If a church does not share the gospel with people and you find yourself having to train them on "evangelism," then stop your training and tell them about Jesus and his Kingdom.

The gospel turns lives upside down. People quit their jobs in business and volunteer with homeless people. A church where the gospel is known is quirky, unpredictable, uncontrollable, uncool, seemingly unstable, and in every way alive. People are loved and the kingdom is built.

[Posted by: fess2]

I think we got it wrong. We say Kingdom of God and gospel. The gospel is defined as good news. The Kingdom of God is a result of that good news and not the good news in and of itself. The Kingdom of God has been defined as either Heaven (eternal life) or as The Bride of Christ coming. Now the gospel is that God has made us a way to heaven through Jesus we can go. It's telling people where they can get a get out of Jail Card—Free!

Is the gospel about me—or is it about God? That's the tension. As people begin to unpackage their faith, they're beginning to question whether there's more to the gospel message than just atonement. Is it about Jesus saving people, or Jesus setting up his kingdom? Postmodernism offers us an opportunity to really wrestle with these questions and risk seeing things in a new light—one that may or may not match our traditional cultural understanding (or our most popular evangelism tools).

[Posted by: liquidthinking]

Going to heaven is not the good news.
Eternal life is not the good news.
Getting out of jail free is not the good news.
Having a personal Lord and Savior is not the good news.
It is a perk.
This is shallow theology resulting from a consumer worldview (i.e., Jesus came to save me). It is not what the Bible says. It says Jesus came to declare the Kingdom of God. That is the good news. Within that is God's redemptive work among many other things.

[Posted by: worshipdude]

It is pretty obvious to me that the Kingdom of God is at hand. God is working through people and relationships....I don't know about you guys, but in the community I live in, this is how God is proclaiming the "good news." It is my experience lately that the church is "being" the church, instead of just inviting people to a building on Sunday to listen to a man they have never heard before in their lives.

Jesus invested time into people's lives....He didn't give them little three-point sermons, some literature, slap 'em on the butt, and call it good. He took the time to touch people, and in turn, people realized how sinful they were. And when this happened, He would look straight into their souls and say, "You don't have to do this anymore.... Come, follow me." That is GOOD NEWS!!!!

[Posted by: footer]

I am discovering (to my wonder, joy, and amazement) that I have mistakenly placed the emphasis of the good news on the eternal. In the Gospels, Jesus wasn't talking about something distant when he proclaimed the good news. It was something for NOW. People could become a part of the Kingdom of God...not a heavenly dwelling but the place where God is King. The place where God turns everything upside down. The place where the light shines and people can be known for who they are and loved. I think I've made the gospel about me, when it's really about God and his Kingdom. It's an invitation for misfits to fit into a thing bigger than themselves. God longs to give his followers the Kingdom. That's the good news. I see a friend struggling with Luke 12 and giving away his possessions, and I see the Kingdom and the good news.

I've lived my Christian life many times with Jesus Christ as an enhancement...thinking that was the good news. "Jesus, come into my life and give me eternal life, plus make my life better." Now I think that's BS and misleading. It eventually leaves me empty at worst and shallow at best. The gospel isn't really about me at all...it's about God and his Kingdom, and an invitation to all to join it.

[Posted by: jaredjohnson]

This gospel isn't an explanation of salvation—it's power. The power of God for salvation. Sometimes we're preaching to people when we should be laying hands on them and healing them. The Holy Spirit empowers us to do the real kingdom stuff. We're not doing God any favors when we, in our flesh, manipulate people and circumstances to get a godly result. If there is no anointing, people will most likely shut you down like they hang up on telemarketers.

One of the criticisms of postmodernism is that it fosters shameless individualism and selfishness, yet this thread would seem to suggest otherwise. Here you have a group of people wanting to put the glory back on God—his purposes and his kingdom. The last post takes this idea even further. We hunger for a story that's bigger than ourselves—one that stretches beyond human effort and includes the mysterious work of the Holy Spirit. If the gospel really is more than salvation, what does this mean for the warrior? What will "success" look like?

Topic: What is successful evangelism?

[Posted by: camd]

I work for a parachurch youth organization that works to feed young people in our community spiritually, emotionally, physically, and relationally. Recently, some coworkers and I were given the responsibility of defining "successful evangelism."

What is successful evangelism?
How do you measure it both in quality and quantity?
How do you know when you've been successful?
How long does it take to be successful?
Does success mean leading someone to pray the "sinner's prayer" or is it a journey of discipleship?
If it is a journey, what is the milestone that marks success?
Are there ministries/organizations/churches that have these measurements defined?
If you define successful evangelism, is it still evangelism, or is it just adding jewels to your crown?

Somehow, we feel we need to know if we are doing what God has called us to do...but the definition of success has become harder to pin down in this postmodern world.

[Posted by: Galadriel]

My personal definition of evangelism involves building relationships with people. I think the best way to lead someone to Jesus Christ is by allowing that person to see, over what could be an extended period of time, the ways God works through your life. I've never been the type of individual whose evangelism encompasses passing out tracts to strangers (not that I'm condemning that method per se).

Successful evangelism is letting God call the shots. Maybe I will be the person that leads these individuals to Jesus Christ or maybe not. Dialogue is the first step. My wiccan, atheist, and agnostic friends know I'm not going to smother anyone with tracts or pressure. Trust is extremely important. I hate nothing more than the feeling that someone is befriending me just so I'll join their church. It needs to be more than that. Evangelism is about caring for individuals as individuals.

[Posted by: dylan]

The Great Commission (Matthew 28:18-20, NRSV):

"All authority in heaven and on earth has been given to me. Go therefore and make disciples of all nations, baptizing them in the

name of the Father and of the Son and of the Holy Spirit, and
teaching them to obey everything that I have commanded you. And
remember, I am with you always, to the end of the age."

Some observations:

1) This commission is not to make churchgoers, adherents of the
Four Spiritual Laws, or any number of other categories. It's not to
make people who are assimilated to our culture or subculture. It's
to make DISCIPLES of Jesus. Discipleship isn't necessarily exclusive
of all of these categories, but we should never mistake other categories for discipleship.

2) This commission involves "teaching them to obey everything that I have
commanded you." I don't think there's any way to do this in a hit-and-run
encounter or via anonymous tracts. It requires ongoing relationship.

Modern evangelism is concerned with success; postmodern evangelism is concerned with process. If your focus is on arriving and getting ahead, then you'll
inevitably need some kind of measurement tools to gauge how well you're doing.
And yet, are numbers appropriate when it comes to evangelism? What does it do
to people, for instance, when their journey is translated into some kind of column
in an annual report? If your measuring stick is, for instance, "exposures to Christ,"
then obviously the more exposures you can get in a year, the better. And yet, what
does a focus on quantity mean for quality?

[Posted by: groovythpstr]

I would say successful evangelism should not just be based on how
many people walk to an altar, say a rehearsed prayer, fill out cards,
join our classes, etc. Salvation is past, present, and future and is a
lot more important than how we have treated it in the past. I really feel awful looking back at times in my life when I had zeal but
lacked knowledge. Inviting Mormons over, listening to their spiel, then
trying to ambush them with Joseph Smith false prophecies.

[Posted by: DesertPastor]

So what have you personally experienced to be more effective? If
your "means" to an end have changed, what does that look like now
to you?

[Posted by: groovythpstr]

Well, from my personal experience, evangelism should be within the
context of both relationship and discipleship. In other words, let's
forget about WWJD bracelets and Christian T-shirts that try to

reduce the mystery of our faith down to a simple slogan. And if we want to talk to Mormons, let's do so with respect and without trying to always prove them wrong. Let's stop trying to force people or argue with people about why we are right because that doesn't really lead anyone into a relationship. Too many times we followers of Jesus Christ come off as arrogant, dogmatic, snotty know-it-alls. It isn't that non-believers don't want anything to do with God; they usually don't want anything to do with us and our darn churches.

[Posted by: suppliants]

Here's one more tidbit of advice for evangelism. Join Amway and spend about a year with them starting up your own "business." Go to their "business" meetings and "business" conferences, listen to their "business" tapes, and watch their instructional "business" videos. Dress as they dress (I hope you don't mind wearing a tie), talk as they talk, swagger as they swagger, talk to everyone about "the business." Now you know what NOT to do in evangelism.

In many ways, we've approached evangelism as an aggressive business venture. The product we're pushing? Jesus. The fact is, if our metaphor changes away from the warrior/aggressive salesman, virtually all of our tools and tactics will need to change. Any curriculum that has been written from the conquering/seal-the-deal mindset will need to be re-written or perhaps thrown out completely. This will be a significant challenge. We know how to teach warriors to fight, but do we know how to train and equip gardeners? It may be that gardening is not taught in a classroom, but instead learned through experience out in the fields of the world.

Thread: What is evangelism?

[Posted by: david33]

I guess my question is a very specific, practical question. Where do I want to direct the conversation? A few years ago, when I was still in seal-the-deal mode, it was easy to know what I was aiming for. The goal was to get the person to accept Jesus Christ. So, as we were talking about life, God, religion, Jesus, etc. (sometimes over several occasions), I would steer the conversation toward a point that presents the other person with a clear choice: either Jesus is important, or he isn't.

If you take away that as the goal, which I think is smart, then what replaces it? On the one hand, I hear people saying just to hang out and help and be a good friend. But on the other hand, the good news is about Jesus, not about friendship. So over a period of months, my friend and I have many conversations relating to inner spiritual issues. Where should I, as a thoughtful Christian, lead that conversation? There may be more than one answer, but it seems like at some point it's got to become a conversation about Jesus.

Doesn't it?

[Posted by: liquidthinking]

Maybe it's not about where you steer the conversation at all. Maybe it's you watching for what God is doing in someone and joining the conversation there.

[Posted by: bigdrink]

I'll borrow from Brian McLaren..."don't count conversions, count conversations." If you concentrate on "sealing the deal" he feels violated, and you nullify the concept of one planting, one watering, and one seals the deal. No one comes to the Father but by the wooing of the Holy Spirit.

[Posted by: ezekiel]

Conversations, not conversions unless it's a van!

[Posted by: charleswear]

I have learned the hard way that the more I "steer" and "direct" the more of a mess I make. Some of the other writers are on the track I would follow. That is, do a lot of listening to your friend and to the Holy Spirit. Mix it with a lot of love and concern. The rest will work itself out, I think....It sounds like your friend needs to know that there is hope for him, that would be really good news, huh?

Throwing away the old formulas—The Four Spiritual Laws, the Romans Road, sharing my testimony—is scary, but formulas can't meet the needs of those who need God....Jesus saved Zacchaeus with an invitation to lunch (and he was inviting himself to Zack's house). The woman at the well was impressed by someone who knew her deepest sin secrets and would still talk to her....Lunches and love, maybe that's the new formula for being a "spiritual friend."

[Posted by: stewie]

Danny DeVito said it very well in the movie The Big Kahuna (a must-see for everyone reading this thread). While talking with a

As was said above, *The Big Kahuna* is the perfect complement to this thread. Should the ends ever justify our means? Is it okay to speak of Jesus Christ's goodness and care for humanity, yet use subversive, manipulative tactics to do it? How has passion clouded our logic? These are the questions people are now daring to ask.

After viewing *The Big Kahuna*, I was struck by how often I too have been a salesman for Jesus. In my evangelistic zeal, I never thought what it must feel like to be on the receiving end of that conversation, and how my desire to seal the deal may have actually been taking away dignity and honor from the person. I frankly didn't realize how important it was to communicate in word and in deed—and for both to be authentic expressions of a changed heart.

[Posted by: mr_magoo]

I had a very "postmodern" conversion experience, so I have a different internal picture of evangelism than most people.

I was raised to believe that all religions were the same and, out
of tolerance, I should accept people with religious views, but I
should look down on them as people who are using a crutch to help
them get through life. It was important to be "good," but without
any real reason for why.

In college, the people I ended up hanging out with were all
Christian. I never once had a discussion about Jesus, though I
heard a few. I never got led into anything. Once, someone (not one
of my friends), tried to have that kind of discussion with me and
it made me defensive and angry. Somehow, somewhere, I moved
from a non-believer to a believer, and I really can't tell you when.

So don't underestimate the power of simply living a life with Jesus
Christ in front of your friend.

I love this post because it answers the question, "Does it work?" If we throw out our tracts, and all our other evangelism "techniques," will people still become followers of Jesus? It seems the answer is yes.

Topic: Leadership in the emerging church?

[Posted by: mr_magoo]

I got to hear Doug Pagitt talk on this topic and because I am the geek of the world, I was taking notes on my Powerbook. It started with Doug pointing out that by using the word "leadership," we are already screwed, because we are uncritically accepting a militaristic model of organization which may not be the healthiest way to build community.

After a long session of people suggesting other models, he suggested the organic gardener, and opened it up to the room to expand on this. Here is what I copied down from the note pad:

Gardener produces healthy fruit, produces life.
Gardeners take crap and use it to nourish things.
It isn't dirt, it is soil. The gardener's highest concern is the soil.
Things that are garbage are used to grow the garden.
Vigilance is important.
Gardener is willing to take smaller fruit in order for it
to be truly healthy.
Gardener requires a systems understanding.
Gardens die every winter and require replanting.
Things can only grow in certain climates. Hybrids don't reproduce.
If you use miracle-grow to start, you have to keep
boosting the amount.
What you plant next to things is what is important.
First piece of effort is preparing the beds.
Gardeners have very little to do with the success of the garden.
Photosynthesis is still a mystery. You can't make it grow;
it is a miracle.
Backs and knees are sore because you are down in the dirt. You
don't stand above the garden.
We need to protect the garden from bunnies. Worms are good, bun-
nies are bad.
Organic fruit doesn't all look like the stuff in the market. Quality
is over beauty, and there is no uniformity.
You share from the excess.

[Posted by: tammy]

---QUOTED---
Gardens die every winter and require replanting.
---END QUOTE---

I love that one. It's not failure. It's the natural life cycle.

These messages further explore the implications of being a gardener in God's kingdom. I love Tammy's post in particular because it draws attention to the fact that changing our mental model will ultimately require a new accompanying vocabulary. Is it failure or is it the natural life cycle? That's a fascinating question and one that challenges all sorts of modern assumptions. Just how much of evangelism is really under our control? How quickly do we expect God to move? Are we willing to wait?

[Posted by: pmatthews]

I think the organic gardener image is good as well. The great thing about the metaphor/simile is that a garden will not grow without a gardener. Translation: you gotta have leadership. It's the way God made things. On the other hand, only God/forces of nature grow a garden. It's total synergy. Seems like I remember some guy writing about someone planting and another watering. Hmm....

[Posted by: odcreech]

Aahhh Father Peter,

I forgot you were on this thing. Yup, synergy. Watering, cultivating, cooperating—good stuff. For analogies (which all break down somewhere), this one is probably the best opportunity of communicating the God kind of leadership in the church as any I have seen.

It seems so many who have left the "traditional" church have simply gotten rid of leadership and have tried to come up with a theology which says there is no need for it. This seems to be a pendulum swing to me too far over. It may be swinging back now, I'm not sure. We need to constantly be making sure we have no wet babies laying in our ecclesiastical yards. Pax et Gratia vobiscum!

[Posted by: moshie]

So much of modern leadership is boxed, one-size-fits-all JUNK.

This is what Eugene Peterson says:

"Why do pastors so often treat congregations with the impatience and violence of developers building a shopping mall instead of the patient devotion of a farmer cultivating a field? The shopping mall will be abandoned in disrepair in fifty years; the field will be healthy and productive for another thousand if its mysteries are respected by a skilled farmer.

"Pastors are assigned by the church to care for congregations, not exploit them, to gently cultivate parishes that are plantings of the Lord, not brashly develop religious shopping malls.

> "No, the congregation is topsoil—seething with energy and organisms that have incredible capacities for assimilating death and participating
>
> in resurrection. The only biblical stance is awe. When we see what is before us, really before us, pastors take off their shoes before the shekinah of congregation."

Moving away from the warrior image is difficult—more difficult, perhaps, than transitioning from any other image. Why? Because playing the role of the warrior comes so naturally to us in our present culture. Many of us have been wearing our armor so long that it now feels normal to us. We barely even notice the weight of it anymore. We're so used to swinging our swords that to do anything else is almost unthinkable. If we weren't warriors in God's army, what would we be?

Yet I can't help but think of Jesus. To be frank, he just wasn't a warrior. In fact, he was anything but. When forced to defend himself before Pilate, he said nothing. He could have done anything he wanted to at that moment, and yet rather than flex his divine muscle, he stood silent. He established his kingdom not by force, but by quiet perseverance. Was he gutless? Hardly. But he didn't use his power to push people around or help him gain another jewel in his crown.

My mission in high school was to claim my campus for Jesus Christ. I very much saw myself as a commando, setting off little evangelistic bombs whenever and wherever I could. The more aggressive I was, the better I felt. Ray, by comparison, was subtle. He just gathered kids together, ate lunch with them and spoke into their lives. "Twelve students" in a classroom—I mean, how effective is that?

I'm being slightly sarcastic, but the point is, we need to peel back our understanding of evangelism and ask if we're really being true to Jesus Christ. What's more, we need to ask how effective we've really been over the years. Has warfare evangelism strengthened the church, or is it beginning to backfire on us? First Peter 3:15 says we need to be ready to "give an answer to everyone who asks you to give the reason for the hope that you have." Could it be that we've been offering answers to questions no one is asking? For many people in our world, the church of Jesus has become an annoying car alarm. It keeps blaring out the message of "turn or burn," but no one wants to listen. Without love, wrote Paul, we're loud gongs and clanging cymbals.

I've always been fascinated by the Great Commission. When you think about it, it's at the core of so much of our evangelistic striving. Why do we need to be out there claiming territory for Jesus? Because he told us to—or did he? I'm not diminishing the importance of sharing our faith, but I do find it fascinating that Jesus' last words differ from gospel to gospel. Take Mark, for instance. After the traditional "Go into all the world" portion is a curious little bit on signs and wonders. Pick up snakes, says Jesus, and you won't be harmed. Drink poison and you'll be fine. Luke, meanwhile, only casually suggests the Great Commission ("You are witnesses of these things," says Jesus) and John—the disciple Jesus loved—doesn't include it at all. What gives? Could it be that we've given too much credence to a particular set of "last words"? Why have we focused so much on proclamation as opposed to, say, living fearlessly in the face of threats from snakes, poison, etc.?

In the church today, we have an opportunity to move forward using a different approach. We have a chance to nurture new growth. That's what is so wonderful about the gardener image. It's not as if gardening is a passive job. It isn't. Not by a long shot. But it isn't aggressive either. It's about caring for people and encouraging them, seeing that they have what they need to sprout and grow. And yet, even in the midst of that care, realizing that growth of any kind is ultimately a mystery. In Mark 4:26–28, we find the parable of the growing seed. "This is what the kingdom of God is like," says Jesus. "A man scatters seed on the ground. Night and day, whether he sleeps or gets up, the seed sprouts and grows, though he does not know how...."

I'm encouraged by the discussion that's happening regarding evangelism in the emerging church. People are beginning to ask these tough questions. They're courageously unpacking their faith even at risk of sounding heretical. Suspicious that our culture may have tainted the gospel and told them only a part of the story, they're going back to the text itself. They're not just looking up proof texts to verify an evangelistic tract. Instead, they're taking a more holistic approach. As postmodern Christians, they're not rejecting absolute truth, but rather questioning whether everything we've held to be completely true really is.

As I ponder the warrior and gardener images, I'm reminded of the prophecies in the Bible that speak of turning swords into plowshares and vice versa (Isaiah 2:4; Micah 4:3; Joel 3:10). As Solomon says in Ecclesiastes, there is a time and season for everything. Is the warrior image biblical? Yes, absolutely. Is the gardener image biblical? Yes, absolutely. The question is determining which image should be guiding us now. I would suggest that now is a time for cultivating graciousness.

Remember when Peter lopped off the servant's ear in the garden? What did Jesus say to him? "Put your sword back in its place, for all who draw the sword will die by the sword. Do you think I cannot call on my Father, and he will at once put at my disposal more than twelve legions of angels? But how then would the Scriptures be fulfilled that say it must happen in this way?" (Matthew 26:52–54). The servant went home that night with two ears firmly in place. Jesus healed him because Peter's move, although passionate and sincere, was out of sync with the purposes of God. You know what? I'm like Peter. Much of my life I've been aggressively evangelizing and swinging my sword in people's faces. But the more the world changes, the more convinced I become that turning my sword into a plowshare may be a better idea for our world today.

Application

1. Where are you on the warrior to gardener continuum?

Warrior	Gardener
• I believe I have the truth and need to proclaim it to others	• I believe I need to live out the truth before people without forcing it on others
• Because I am at odds with the world, I need to take territory for Jesus and see light triumph over darkness	• Because I have a lot in common with people, I can care for them and be "present" with them no matter what their worldview
• Because time is limited, I need to hurry and help people make a decision	• Because I believe in seasons, I can be patient with people and trust God to change their hearts

2. Think of a person who has had a strong influence in your life. Was he or she a gardener or a warrior?

3. How might your relationships change if you were to become more like a gardener?

A Metaphor for
LIFE

Chapter 9

In Chapter 1, I talked about the importance of mental models—how the pictures in our heads affect how we interact with the world. We've also spent several chapters exploring how various metaphors impact the way we "do" church—things like ministry and missions, for instance. While I trust you've found these ideas helpful, I think perhaps this last chapter may be the most valuable of all—particularly as you sort through what postmodernism means for your own personal journey.

The question is, what metaphor is guiding your life? How do you view your calling and your purpose? How do you see yourself?

What's your metaphor?

I don't know about you, but I've filled in more than my fair share of personality tests and spiritual gift inventories over the years. To be honest, I've never found them all that helpful. The problem, I think, is that they take a very literal, analytical approach. "Oh, you like X, Y, and Z? Well, that means you're this personality type. And here's how you should be living your life."

That kind of labeling has never worked for me. The descriptions are sometimes close, but never bang on. I felt trapped more than anything. Being put in a category didn't seem to spur me on or help me take the next steps. Then I discovered the power of metaphor. You know what I see myself as now? Kindling. Before I'm a gardener, or a warrior, or a teacher, or any other metaphor in this book, I'm kindling. I'm that little bundle of sticks that get things started. I can come into a situation and create instant energy. On the flipside, I can also burn out quickly, so it's important for me to pace myself and surround myself with people who can burn long and bright.

In the modern world, we tend to identify ourselves by positions, roles, and titles. Ask someone to talk about themselves and what do they inevitably say? "Oh, I'm an accountant," or "I'm a pastor." They talk about their professions. It's the same at church. We spell out our particular denominational affiliation. "I'm a Baptist," or "Oh, I'm a Methodist." We're obsessed with labels. Metaphor has the power to help us identify ourselves in new, boundary-breaking ways—ways that facilitate conversation and help us relate to each other as individuals, not stereotypes.

I remember talking to my friend Bruce about the life metaphor concept. A commercial realtor by profession, he was leery of the idea. Let's face it, when your whole life is about numerical calculations, it's hard to make the switch to warm, fuzzy images. Still, Bruce persevered. He agreed to go home and think about what image best represented who he was and who he was called to be. The next week, I visited Bruce at his office. On the side of his desk, was a small red vice with two googly eyes on top. The clamp was holding a few papers.

"I'm somebody who holds things together," Bruce explained, smiling. "I'm not a big vice—I don't crush people—but I do know how to apply pressure. I also know when to let go."

For some reason, the vice image resonated with Bruce in a way all kinds of written descriptions and categories on worksheets had not. Eight years later, he still talks about what a breakthrough that was for .

As I think about what it will take to move forward in our spiritual journeys, I think self-awareness will be key. Before we can change the church (or even the metaphors of the church), we need to understand who we are as individuals and what we bring to the table. Can you imagine going to a party and saying, "I'm a vice"? And yet, that's exactly what it will take to move forward in this postmodern culture. We need to learn a new way of approaching life.

Learning to walk again

When I was in my junior year of high school, I was hit by a car in front of my church. I'd been out taking photographs of the church for our new directory when—WHAM—I was hit squarely in the back by a car traveling 35 MPH. I was thrown sixty-three feet.

My injuries were serious. So serious, in fact, that the paramedics weren't sure I'd even make it to the hospital. I had three damaged vertebrae in my lower back, a severe concussion, and a leg twisted like a pretzel. The elders came, lined the hallway of the emergency room, and prayed.

When I came to, the doctors told me that I might walk again, but that it would be an uphill battle. Physical therapy was a daily nightmare of pain. After a while, I could pull myself through a six-foot length of parallel bars. It was a great start, but there was still much progress to be made.

One day, a few weeks after I'd been released from the hospital, I was still covered in scabs and dependent on a walker. While riding in the car with my mother, I noticed a guy jogging. He wasn't a great runner, but his body was moving rhythmically. His arms, legs, back, and head were all in motion…working together. At that moment, I realized I would probably never again enjoy the freedom of movement this jogger was taking for granted.

I began screaming at my mother to turn the car around and head for home. We'd been on our way to a doctor's appointment, but I no longer wanted to go. I was done with physical therapy. I was done with pain. I was done with all of it. I didn't care if I ever walked again.

Ignoring my cursing and sobbing, my mother kept going. When the doctor came in to see me, he was far less gentle than usual. During the flexibility test, he grabbed my knee and pushed my heel level with the floor. A blood-curdling scream filled the office. I looked down. The leg I thought would never be the same was actually the same length as the other. My doctor looked me square in the eye: "If you want to, you can walk again, but only if you learn in a new way."

The fact is, learning to walk in new ways is painful. The fear of failure is always there, as is the desire to limp along and deny reality.

In many ways, the shift from modern to postmodern culture is a bit like being hit by a car. You're not sure where you are, what's happened, or how to move forward. In my own experience, embracing metaphor has been a significant part of the healing process. It's even enabled me to see the world in a new way—filled with new opportunities.

For twenty years, I took the Bible very literally. I assumed, for example, that "Go into all the world" (Mark 16:15) meant exactly that. Take geography for Jesus. The past few years, I've begun to see "the world" is bigger than the 10/40 window. Many people live behind the 640 x 480 window—and experience the world through a computer screen.

The postmodern culture in which we live has a different language and different ways of doing things. Consequently, I'm learning to walk again in a different way—a way outside the confines of traditional ministry and spirituality. I've come to appreciate that Paul's missionary journeys were into other cultures, not just into specific cities. Remember when Paul said, "I have become all things to all people so that by all possible means I might save some. I do all this for the sake of the gospel" (1 Corinthians 9:22)? I can't help but think he means holding everything loosely—and being the gospel in our world.

Getting out of the tank

Perhaps as you've read this book, you have felt overwhelmed by many of the thoughts and ideas suggested. Perhaps you've doubted whether you could really learn to walk in this new way and persevere through the pain required to get there. I understand those feelings. Believe me, I do.

Five years ago, I quit my job at a dream church to become a tentmaker of sorts. I gave up the security of my air-conditioned office and regular paycheck to spend each day in my garage-turned-office, creating something called TheOoze.com— an online community devoted to discovering what it means to be an authentic follower of Jesus in a postmodern world.

It hasn't been an easy transition, that's for sure. And yet, I know it's what I'm called to. After all, I'm kindling, remember? I start things. I help spread the flame to other people.

No matter where you're at, I think the important thing is not to hinder the progress of other people. Find ways to support them in their healing journey—no matter what it looks like. Do you know someone who's starting an organic church or trying some other way of bringing the gospel to your community in a non-traditional way? Consider how you can support them in that effort—even if it's not the way you'd do it.

I think back to my days as a youth pastor. About sixteen years into it, I realized I needed to replace myself. Frankly, I was getting too old for the job. So bit by bit, I developed a plan to move on. I set up an internship program, gathered all kinds of young and capable volunteers, and prepared to pass the reins. Then the strangest thing happened. One Sunday I took up my usual spot in the baptismal tank (the church practiced full immersion) and suddenly realized I didn't need to be there. Although I'd worked with the kids for years, I hadn't actually been a part of the baptism class. My two associates—Keith and Gary—had run the sessions and they were the ones the kids wanted to have do the honors. It was surreal. I literally had to get out of the tank and stand to the side while teen after teen took the jubilant plunge.

It was strange. My desire had been for Keith and Gary to connect with the kids and be a part of their lives in significant ways, and yet there I was—feeling sad about it. I mourned the fact that I had been replaced. At the same time, though, I celebrated the expansion of the kingdom.

As I see it, we have at least two choices as Christians living in a postmodern world. We can learn to walk in new, different ways for the sake of the gospel. Or we can step out of the baptismal tank and cheer others on in their journey. But we have to do something….

About the Authors

Spencer Burke

A former pastor and accomplished photographer, Spencer Burke is the creator of TheOoze.com, a Web site focusing on issues facing the emerging church. He is also the founder of ETREK.com, an innovative experiential learning program connecting leaders in the local church with those at the forefront of the emerging church conversation. Spencer is a well-known speaker and the host of Soularize: A Learning Party—a national gathering of traditional and non-traditional theologians, church planters, artists, and musicians.

Before getting involved in the emerging church dialogue, Spencer spent twenty-two years in traditional ministry environments, serving in a variety of denominations. Most recently, he spent eight years at Mariners Church in Irvine, California, and has served the past four years on the board of elders at ROCKharbor Church in Costa Mesa, California. Spencer is a founding board member of the Damah Film Festival, an annual competition celebrating spiritual experiences in film.

Spencer is married to Lisa and they live in a small 1920s BeachShack in Newport Beach, California. They have two children, Alden (age six) and Grace (two).

Colleen Pepper

Colleen completed her Bachelor of Arts degree in communications and history at Trinity Western University, Langley, British Columbia. She spent three years working as a staff writer for a large parachurch organization before launching her own communications firm, Pepper Creative (www.peppercreative.ca), in 2001.

She and her husband Jeremy live in Vancouver, British Columbia, and attend a small Presbyterian church—a mission to one of the most unchurched areas in North America.

Online Resources

TheOoze.com
Conversation for the Journey

Join more than 100,000 unique users from ninety different countries on TheOoze.com—the site that started it all.

Share your hopes, dreams, fears, and frustrations. Interact with LiquidThinking, ChickenFriedFunk, and others from *Making Sense of Church* on TheOoze message board. It's time to add your voice to the mix.

With thought-provoking articles and a host of other resources, TheOoze.com gives you the insight you need on the issues facing the emerging church. Become part of a vibrant online community that will challenge and encourage you in your journey.

We hope to see you online today at www.TheOoze.com.

ETREK.com
Learning Journeys

Ready to go deeper? ETREK is a six-month course connecting leaders in the local church with those at the forefront of the emerging church conversation. Connect with Leonard Sweet, Sally Morganthaler, Brian McLaren, Todd Hunter, and other key leaders.

ETREK learning groups are made up of fourteen students from all over North America, plus a facilitator. There are many topcs to choose from, and ETREK groups include both online and offline learning. Phone conferences with cutting-edge thinkers and facilitated discussions with your peers will challenge you to go deeper in your thinking. You'll have an opportunity to really wrestle with issues and then celebrate that learning with others.

ETREK makes learning personal and interactive—it's experiential, not just educational.

To find out more, log on to www.ETREK.com or call (949) 631–0104.

MakingSenseOfChurch.com
Beyond the Book

You've read the book. Now log on to the *Making Sense of Church* Web site to continue the conversation!

With a message board for each metaphor featured in this book, MakingSenseOfChurch.com gives you a chance to dive in and discuss what you've read with others. Offer your feedback. Share your life metaphor. Read what others are saying. Contribute new ideas.

Looking for some more concrete examples of the metaphors in action? At MakingSenseOfChurch.com, you'll find inspirational stories of individuals and communities who are breaking the rules and experiencing incredible vitality as a result.

Thinking of studying *Making Sense of Church* with your small group? Check out our special group purchase rates and downloadable discussion guides. There's also an expanding resource list.

It's all online at www.MakingSenseofChurch.com.

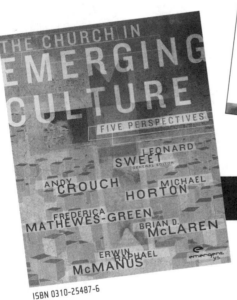

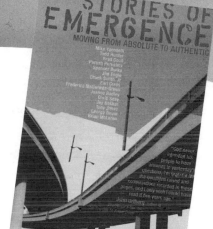